The Japanese Arts
and Self-Cultivation

The Japanese Arts
and Self-Cultivation

Robert E. Carter

Foreword by
Eliot Deutsch

State University of New York Press

Published by
State University of New York Press, Albany

© 2008 State University of New York

All rights reserved

Printed in the United States of America

No part of this book may be used or reproduced in any manner whatsoever
without written permission. No part of this book may be stored in a retrieval system
or transmitted in any form or by any means including electronic, electrostatic,
magnetic tape, mechanical, photocopying, recording, or otherwise
without the prior permission in writing of the publisher.

For information, contact State University of New York Press, Albany, NY
www.sunypress.edu

Production by Diane Ganeles
Marketing by Anne M. Valentine

The cover photo is a partial view of Masuno Shunmyo's "Zen Garden" at the Canadian
Museum of Civilization in Ottawa, Canada. It is called WAKEI NO NIWA, which means to
understand and respect all cultures. The photo was taken by Robert E. Carter.

Library of Congress Cataloging-in-Publication Data

Carter, Robert Edgar, 1937–
    The Japanese arts and self-cultivation / Robert E. Carter ; foreword by
Eliot Deutsch.
        p. cm.
    Includes bibliographical references and index.
    ISBN 978-0-7914-7253-8 (hardcover : alk. paper) — ISBN 978-0-7914-7254-5
(pbk. : alk. paper) 1. Arts, Japanese. 2. Spirituality—Japan. 3. Japan—
Civilization—Philosophy. I. Title.

NX584.C36   2007
700.952—dc22

2006101108

10 9 8 7 6 5 4 3 2 1

Dedicated to my beloved family:

Deanie
Scott
Meredith
Rob
and Emerson

CONTENTS

FOREWORD

Robert E. Carter has written an extremely informative and subtle account of the role of the arts in the Japanese tradition as they relate primarily to the ethical orientation and religious values of the Japanese people. The work is written with great clarity and exhibits a sensitive understanding of and often very original take on what for many Westerners is a culture buried in exquisite obscurities. Without in any way denying the profound mysteries that inform traditional Japanese art, Carter makes perfectly clear and evident the integral way in which the training in any of the arts is at the same time the crafting of a certain ethical attitude that informs one's entire manner of being in the world.

The Japanese Arts and Self-Cultivation is aimed primarily for nonspecialists in Japanese culture. Nevertheless, the work presents a number of insightful interpretations of key Japanese aesthetic and metaphysical concepts, such as *yūgen* and *ki*, that a specialist can fruitfully engage. One of the most effective achievements of Carter's work, I believe, is the way in which he is able to explicate and weave together philosophical background notions with detailed descriptions of the intricacies of the various arts that he explored. The first chapter of the book is devoted to a careful philosophical discussion of, for example, the meaning of the idea of the "bodymind," (the functional inseparability of the mental and the physical), *shugyō*, or continual practice and training, and theories of artistry.

Carter interprets the meaning of the various arts in Japan as Ways (*dō*) or disciplines involving a self-cultivating practice that aims to achieve a form of *satori* or enlightenment, one that will allow for a certain openness and ethical sensitivity to others and to the world. Carter characterizes ethics (in "the broadest sense") as "those attitudes which are significant in the way one lives one's life, both alone and with others." In moral education, he writes, "one learns the rules early on, but as one matures as a person, it is not the rules that keep one on the ethical path, it is the transformation that has taken place in one's personality that now spontaneously responds to situations with a benevolent heart." This path of moral development parallels, in aesthetic terms, exactly the training and development of the master artist. This is not surprising as the aesthetic and the ethical are, for Carter, intimately interrelated.

In Western philosophical aesthetics, Kant perhaps came closet to the East Asian understanding of the relationship between the aesthetic and the ethical when he insisted that aesthetic sensitivity toward the beautiful could lead quite naturally to the kind of impartiality he thought was required for the ethical. But how incredible it would be to imagine Kant closing a chapter on landscape gardening with a section entitled "The Ethics of Gardens." Carter would likely, and I believe rightly, say, "Too bad for Kant!"

The artistic practices or Ways that Carter focuses on in his work are *aikidō*, understood not so much as a martial art, but as a practice seeking harmony and peace; landscape gardening which is a way of attaining a sense of interconnectedness with and respect for all things; the Zen-influenced Tea ceremony, flower arrangement, and pottery, with also numerous references to poetry and painting, all of which are regarded as disciplines that strengthen the bodymind and transform the artist into a whole person.

Carter's work is indeed a celebration of the spiritual possibilities of art and is written in a manner that is at once philosophically sophisticated and personally engaging. He relates many interviews he had with master artists in Japan, experiences he had on trains where his fellow passengers guide him to the beauty of what can be seen in the passing countryside, and so on.

I first read the manuscript of *The Japanese Arts and Self-Cultivation* with an eye to preparing this foreword. I intend now to read the book a second time for the sheer joy of doing so.

—ELIOT DEUTSCH

ACKNOWLEDGMENTS

I am deeply grateful to the Japan Foundation for a Fellowship that took me to Japan to consult with various artists and philosophers about their life's work. Trent University's Research Committee has also supported the research and writing of this book, for which I offer my thanks.

To the following persons who gave of their time to respond to my queries about their art and themselves, I offer my heartfelt thanks: Tohei Shinichi, Deputy President, Ki no Kenkyukai International, Clayton Naluai (Lokahi Ki Aikidō, Honolulu), Christopher Curtis and Suzuki Shinichi (Maui Ki Aikidō Society), and David E. Shaner, seventh dan (*aikidō*) and Okuden (*ki*), Chief Instructor, Eastern Ki Federation and Gordon Poteat Professor of Philosophy and Asian Studies, Furman University, for *aikidō*; Masuno Shunmyo and Masuno Yoshihiko (Kenko-ji Temple, Yokohama) and Allen M. Reid, University of Ottawa, for landscape gardening; Dr. Sen Genshitsu (Urasenke School of Tea, Kyoto) and Teruko Sofu Shin (Toronto) for the Way of Tea; Inoue Manji (Arita, Kyushu), potter and Living National Treasure; Miura Eiko, international teacher, and Kenneth Jones, Section Chief, International Events, Ikenobo Headquarters in Kyoto, for the Ikenobo School of Flower Arranging; Hata Masataka (Shoyeido Incense Company, Kyoto) for the Way of Incense (*kodō*); in Yagyu, Hashimoto-sensei, head priest of Hotokuzen-ji, Hasegawa Hideko (Bōjutsu master), and Ichiba Tomiko (Naginata master); Dr. Motoyama Hiroshi, Shintō priest and founder of the California Institute for Human Sciences (CIHS); H. E. Davey (Director of the Sennin Foundation Center for Japanese Cultural Arts, San Francisco); and Professor Yuasa Yasuo, (Professor of Japanology and Director of International Studies at Obirin University, Tokyo) regarding the theory of self-cultivation and many other matters. These grand people, and many others who helped during my stay in Japan, have been central in bringing my work to this tentative conclusion.

Several individuals also helped enormously as interpreters and translators: Professor Reiko Aiura of Shiga University; Professor Emeritus Toshi Hisama, now retired from Kansai Gaidai University, in Kyushu; Professor Yasuhiro Enomoto, Professor of Linguistics, Kansai Gaidai University; Hiroshi Canbara, graduate student at Kansai Gaidai; Kaori Maruya, graduate student at Kansai Gaidai; and Vlad Tokan, of the Urasenke School of Tea. All of these people made clear what might otherwise have remained obscure.

To Professor Eliot Deutsch, Chair of Philosophy at the University of Hawaii at Manoa, I owe a special thanks for having undertaken to write the foreword to this book. His work spans Eastern and Western philosophy, and aesthetics and ethics, to metaphysics and epistemology. I was hopeful that he would agree to write the foreword, for his broad understanding of comparative philosophy, art, and life made him the ideal person to set the stage for my study.

Finally, my thanks to my wife, Deanie LaChance, teacher and family therapist, and Professor Sean Kane of Trent University, a specialist in English and Cultural Studies, for reading this manuscript and making countless suggestions for improvement. Jerry Larock, a former student and a black belt martial artist, read the manuscript several times, making countless suggestions and numerous corrections, and helped with the index. Their insight has made of this book far more than it might have been without their critical input. Please know how much I appreciate the hours given to this project.

Introduction

Art, philosophy, and religion are intertwined in Japanese culture, entangled like grapevines on an old wooden trellis. This book attempts to capture something of the complexity of this intertwining, and to relate it to ethics: how it is learned, and how it is lived. There is very little systematic writing in Japan about Japanese ethics and the ethical. This is because Japanese ethics is usually studied as an aspect of Buddhist or Confucian thought. The indigenous religion, Shintō, in which so much of Japanese cultural expression has its grounding, is for the most part ignored altogether with respect to the study of ethics, because it has no texts and no teachings to draw upon. Stuart Picken observes that "Shintō is indeed a religion that is 'caught' rather than 'taught,' its insights 'perceived' before they are 'believed,' its basic concepts 'felt' rather than 'thought'" (Picken 1994, 45). And some of those basic concepts and attitudes that are taken in with one's mother's milk, so to speak, inform ethics in Japan. They are taught indirectly rather than directly, "caught" rather than "taught," emulated rather than theorized about or memorized as rules to assiduously follow.

Japanese ethics, then, is derived from Shintō, Buddhist, and Confucian sources, and as will be seen, from Zen Buddhism as well, the distinctively Japanese form of Buddhism. In a previous book, I investigated the details of these influences on ethics in Japan (Carter 2001). What I briefly explored in that study was how ethics was not taught simply in the temples, in the schools,

---

A Note to the Reader: All quotations without source, year, and page number are from interviews with masters and teachers which I conducted in Japan in September and October of 2003. The context makes clear who is speaking.

1

and in the home, but also through the remarkably distinctive arts of Japan, including the martial arts. Consequently, my working hypothesis for this book was that ethics is primarily taught through the various arts, and is not learned as an abstract theory, or as a series of rules to remember. Even today, young women in Japan still study at least one of the arts, even if only briefly. Many young men and an increasing number of women are involved in the martial arts. But whether most engage in the practice of the arts or not, the influence of the arts on Japanese culture remains strong. Nō drama, flower arranging, the Tea ceremony, the many martial arts, poetry (especially haiku poetry), pottery, landscape gardening and design, *sumi-e* painting, paper making, the incense ceremony, calligraphy, and even traditional dance and music, among other forms, continue to exert strong influence on the culture in films, literature, on television, and through numerous demonstrations attracting large crowds. The interest in these arts has certainly declined in recent years, with the possible exception of the martial arts. Nonetheless, many of these arts are once more being taught as part of the school curriculum. Each has strong instructional centers, and even universities where "masters" are on hand to model the aims and achievements of the art. As well, the tradition of selecting "Living National Treasures" further ties the arts to Japanese culture. No more than seventy Living National Treasures are designated at any one time, each artist demonstrating the highest excellence in his or her art or craft, while apprenticing at least three novices to ensure that the artistic skills and basic outlooks are handed on. To anyone interested in one of the arts, the name of a Living National Treasure representing that art is virtually a household name. In fact, they have something of the standing that is attached to sports heroes, Hollywood stars, or pop culture idols.

Some years ago, I journeyed to the pottery town of Mashiko to visit the potter Hamada Shoji,[1] himself a Living National Treasure. I arrived in the town, quite early in the morning. Hamada's rural compound was several kilometers from the station, and I asked a taxi driver to take me there, and was about to hand him the map

---

1. Readers should be aware that I will adhere to the Far Eastern tradition of placing the surname first, followed by the personal name or names. On occasion I will break this rule when an individual is already well known in the West by his surname placed last.

that had been prepared for me, identifying the complex route to his pottery. Excitedly, the white-gloved driver exclaimed "Hamada!" in a loud voice, and then bowed deeply, showing respect for this potter of renown, even here in Mashiko where everybody is a potter. He waved off the written directions, opened the door of the taxi for me, and we set off to find Hamada's residence and pottery. When we arrived, the staff member who greeted me was also greeted with respect, and I left my driver continuing to bow to me, to the staff member and to the yet-invisible Hamada as we made our way to his studio. I have had similar experiences when inquiring about other highly respected artists in Japan. An aura of respect and awe surrounds them, even when they are merely mentioned by name.

The arts of Japan contribute in hundreds of subtle ways to the transmission of Japanese culture, remaining collectively a significant repository of culture and tradition. However, the repository contains not only artistic themes and skills but philosophical understanding. By "philosophical understanding" I mean the proper attitudinal stances to be taken in the living of one's life and in the religious practices that are meant to lead to self-transformation, and ethical teachings concerning how one should relate to other people, to nature, and to the cosmos. The great difference that needs to be understood is that these artistic "Ways" (Japanese *dō*) are unlike sports, or hobbies, or even vocational and commercial activities as we know them in the West. Each of the arts is a pathway, a road, which is what *dō* means, from the Chinese *tao* or *dao*, and it also signifies a way of life, as in *aikidō*, *judō*, *chadō*, and so forth. None of these is to be understood and undertaken merely as entertainment or distraction: they are all ways of self-development, leading to a transformation of who a person is. In short, each of these arts, if seriously engaged in, is itself enlightenment in some form.

The word commonly associated with the required lifelong practice of a "Way" is *shugyō*.[2] It is never a casual undertaking but an ultimately serious journey as some form of spiritual awakening,

---

2. *Shugyō* is a term that applies to rigorous, dedicated, long-term or life-long practice. *Keiko* refers to shorter-term practice, or even a single session, and while it may demand the "total exertion" that Zen Master Dōgen (1200–1253) refers to when he demands the full use of all of one's dimensions, body, mind, and spirit, it need not. *Shugyō*, by definition, is always a sustained and spiritual undertaking stretching over a lifetime.

or realization. There is nothing like this understanding in the West, which does not employ its arts and crafts, or its sports, to teach the deepest religious and ethical truths of its culture. Some of the latter are found in sports, as in the values called sportsmanship, or being a team player, and so on, but Westerners do not engage in sports to achieve spiritual self-transformation. In contrast, the Japanese arts are intended to immerse one in the highest achievements, the most noble aspirations, and the meditational techniques needed to take one to these heights and ideals through diligent and lifelong practice. Rather than taking the "average" as the standard in assessing what human beings are capable of, "the traditional Eastern pattern of thinking takes as its standard people who have acquired a higher capacity than the average person through rigorous training" (Yuasa 1993, 61). This approach seeks out ways of restoring the original mind-body unity by investigating "exceptional cases such as, for example, a genius or the masters of various disciplines" (Yuasa 1993, 61). This results in a change in meaning, for the "normal" is no longer based on a large number of cases, or the majority, so that whatever does not fit the "norm" is "abnormal." Instead, the large majority come to be thought of as "abnormal," and the exceptional are the ones who provide the standard of what human beings are capable of becoming. However, to become what we are capable of becoming requires diligent and long-term practice: *shugyō*. The arts are designed to lead an individual to realize Buddhahood, or to release one's *kami*-nature, the divine potential that is to be found in the depths of each and every individual who cares to discover it. Religion, philosophy, aesthetics, culture, and ethics are all interconnected here. The practice of a Japanese art is in all respects transformative. Each art is designed to make one a different person, a better person (that is to say, one closer to the standard), and one is able to practice what has come to be understood. True understanding is never just theory in Japan, but everyday practice.

However, while ethics in the Japanese sense is an ever-present theme of this book, weaving in and out of discussions of the arts themselves, the "ethics" depicted is not "ethics" in the modern Western sense. Ethics in modern and contemporary Western philosophy has been a search for the criterion or criteria of right and wrong actions. For the most part, at least until quite recently, the old Aristotelian sense of ethics as character development has been pushed aside, and "meta-ethical" questions about the meaning of terms such as "good" and "bad," "right" and "wrong," "action" and "intention" have taken center stage. Consequentialists of various stripes (who hold that it is the *consequences* of actions that determine rightness and wrongness), and deontologists (who hold that certain *kinds* of actions are right or wrong, such as promise keeping) have battled it out in an attempt to discern that criterion or criteria by means of which correct ethical decision making can occur.

By contrast, ethics in Japan has rarely dealt with such matters and instead has focused on the development of character and of the whole person. Correct ethical action most often grows out of concrete, physical training, or repetition, and is best described as a cluster of attitudes about who one is in the world and how to properly and effectively interact with others. Ethics is not a theoretical, intellectual "meta" search, but a way of walking (or being) in the world. It is a recognition that we are not only inextricably intertwined with others but with the entire cosmos. This "declaration of interdependence" is the basis of all ethical action: if I am one with my brothers and sisters, then it is as unthinkable to do any of them harm intentionally as it is to do harm to myself. Enlightenment is the experience of this oneness, and enlightenment is inevitably the "goal" that is sought in the various practices. Enlightenment is an important realization along the pathways of diligent practice, but all along the path, glimpses of the unfolding of enlightenment are present. Enlightenment is not separate from practice, but is everywhere present, even though it is, at the same time, an achievement (or a series of achievements) that offers a level of realization not heretofore fully comprehended. In this way, ethics in Japan is not separate from the arts, or from the practice of religion, or from the everyday living of one's life. Ethics is a way of being in the world, a comprehensive sense of the oneness of things that yields a joy in living as fully as possible with others and in nature.

In what follows I examine several of the arts and attempt to draw out the teachings that most relate to ethics, understood in the Japanese sense. By that I mean those attitudes that are significant in the way one lives one's life, both alone and with others. It will be difficult to strictly brand any of these ways as utilitarian, or deontological, or virtues oriented, although one might do this in something of a casual way. Instead, what will emerge is a picture of a human being that is capable of the highest interpersonal ideals, while at the same time living a life of personal joy and fulfillment. When I asked a teaching master of tea what she learned from making tea, she replied, "I have learned to be happy, everyday, all day." The look on her face, and the fact that she was still teaching well into her declining years, convinced me of the authenticity of her claim.

There is a favorite Zen story of an arrogant man who comes to a Zen master for instruction, making clear what it is that he needs in no uncertain terms. The Zen master, having invited him to tea, continues to pour tea into his cup long after it is full. The prospective student complains that the cup is already full, and the master responds that like the tea bowl, one who is already full will be quite unable to learn anything. In ethics, too, one who is full will be unable to respond to the other, whether person or thing, by listening carefully before acting. Being empty is the first step in being truly open to the other, and being open to the other is to be unified with the other by being the other alone, for a moment, in the forgetting of oneself and attending fully to that other. Perhaps this is the heart of ethics in Japan: they teach how to be in the world, alone and with others, becoming the other, in the moment, in the now, in this place where the world is just now unfolding. And this is what the arts teach, in so many different ways, but with astounding ability and patience.

CHAPTER ONE

Self-Cultivation

Whenever one looks at ideas and concepts translated from another culture, the seemingly familiar language may contain implications that are quite different from one's own tradition. Surely one must ask how many of our assumptions must be jettisoned if genuine understanding is to be achieved. Furthermore, how is it possible to know whether one has, in fact, abandoned one's own presuppositions such that one is actually grasping the intended meanings in translation? The strength of our own presuppositions may actually override the genuine differences in play. Difficult as it may be to "read" another culture, the struggle to clarify can move us closer to grasping cultural differences, as well as similarities. An open-minded approach yields something of a fusion of horizons, at the very least, whereby one is forever changed by differences in approach, meaning, and life stance. To the extent that each of us will allow, our horizon of understanding merges with that of another culture resulting in a new and exciting way of looking at both their horizon and our own.

In engaging in the cross-cultural dialogue of this study, there are five key concepts that require some clarification to bring us as close as possible to speaking the same language, with minimal distortion. These five concepts are: (1) the bodymind and the unification of mind and body; (2) enlightenment; (3) meditation; (4) self-transformation (self-cultivation); and (5), *ki* energy. There is an excellent illustration of the importance of striving to ensure that the words in one cultural language are correctly translated into the appropriate words of another culture in the following dialogue that I had with Masuno Shunmyo, a Zen Buddhist landscape architect. The subject matter seemed straightforward enough, for it concerned the nature of the "mind."

7

The Bodymind

Kenkoh-ji Temple, in Yokohama, Japan, is a quiet sanctuary in a busy neighborhood. The main temple hall is traditional in design and is now connected to a building that is quite modern. It was there that I waited to meet with Masuno Shunmyo. A Sōtō Zen Buddhist priest and head priest of Kenkoh-ji, he is also one of Japan's most distinguished landscape garden designers, one who still creates in accordance with traditional Zen Buddhist design principles. He has an international reputation, and his gardens "live" in many parts of the world. Chapter 3, further on, deals with Masuno and his work in greater detail. Here I only wish to make use of one of his comments in order to help lay the groundwork for what is to follow in this study.

Our discussion began in a simple meeting room adjacent to the main temple hall over a cup of green tea, and Masuno quickly affirmed that his designs are "expressions of [his] mind." The startling insight that he provided at the outset was the placing of his hand over his heart, in order to seal with a gesture the location of the "mind." I smiled broadly and remarked that most Western people would be surprised to see the heart identified as the seat of the mind. He and his assistant were surprised by this implicit critique of the obvious, and asked where the mind was thought to be located. "We would point to the head, to the brain," I replied, causing a moment of disbelief. "Why would anyone think that the mind was located in the head?" he asked politely.

A few weeks later, this scenario was repeated in conversation with two of the world leaders in the practice of the martial art of *aikidō* at the World Camp gathering that brings together each year a hundred or more of the most skilled *aikidōka* in the world. The camp was in Toshigi Prefecture, north of Tokyo, and I was honored with an opportunity to interview Tohei Shinichi, the son of the now elderly and ill founder of the Ki Society School of *aikidō*, together with a philosopher and holder of a black belt of high rank, Professor David Edward Shaner of Furman University. *Aikidō* will be one of the main subjects of chapter 2, where I will deal with *aikidō* generally and with the Ki Society in particular. At this meeting, we were discussing the spiritual and ethical implications of *aikidō*, when the subject of the nature and location of the mind came up. Tohei Shinichi (the son) placed his hand on the left side of his chest and continued to speak of the mind as that faculty which leads the body in its activities. I remarked that what he took for granted with regard to the location of the "mind" contrasted sharply with the West's assumption that the mind is in the head, directly associated with the brain. Again, there was shock and disbelief that anyone would assume that the mind was associated with the head, rather than focused in the heart and manifest over the entire body. Tohei Shinichi then turned to Professor Shaner, saying "now I understand why you had to coin the term 'bodymind' in order to emphasize what is meant by the oneness of mind and body." Thus, it comes as no surprise, theoretically speaking, to find the Japanese understanding of the mind/body relationship to be quite different from the philosophical traditions of the West.

It was the philosopher René Descartes (1596–1650) in the West who solidified the radical separation of mind and body. Descartes wrote of the mind as a spiritual substance, whose essential characteristic was the ability to think. He divided the world into two kinds of objects: those which are extended in space, and those which are thinking things. The essential qualities of these two classes of things are mutually exclusive: bodies do not think, only minds do; and minds are not extended in space, only bodies are. The problem this left him was how something immaterial and nonspatial could have an effect on something nonthinking and material. Whatever mind is, it is not material like a body, and whatever body is, it is not mindlike in any way. The difficulties tied to trying to explain how two radically different things, mind and body, can interact, is still studied in philosophy courses as "the mind/body problem."

By contrast, Thomas P. Kasulis writes that "Asian traditions typically do not sharply separate the mind from the body. Although the mind and body may be conceptually distinguishable from some perspectives, they are not assumed to be ontologically distinct" (Yuasa 1987, 1). The Japanese word *kokoro* means both "mind" and "heart," where heart refers to the affective dimension of awareness, which is, of course, situated in the body, and the significance of a single term serving to identify both mind and heart is that it blurs the distinction between the two. In the Japanese language, mind and heart are one, and the metaphorical seat of the mind is the heart, and, thus, "mind" [*kokoro*], as ordinarily understood in Japanese, is inclusive of both reason and emotion, both thinking and feeling.

Mind and body are everywhere intertwined, and it is in abstract thinking alone that we find them separated. The modern problem in the West has been how to put the two back together again. Abstract reason erected a radical gulf between the two which Western civilization has been seeking to bridge for centuries. However, mind and body are, and always have been, two sides of the same coin. Heads and tails do not need to be linked, for they are already one. The two sides can be distinguished, as can the edge, but together they form or constitute a single coin. And like a coin, we, too, are one, and not at all in need of being put back together again like Humpty Dumpty. Of course, one might ask why, if the two were never actually separated, it is necessary to reconnect them. It is one thing to resist separating mind and body conceptually, however, and another to learn how to act with mind/body oneness in whatever one does. Practitioners of *aikidō* and most Japanese philosophers insist that bodymind unity is our natural state, but we have forgotten this and have learned to treat the two as separate. We must keep in mind a distinction between the ego (the everyday mind) and the deeper self (the "true" self) which represents who we really are. At this deeper level, body and mind are one, but at the level of the ego, which is the reasoning self, we conceive of the material world as separate from us. Our bodies, as part of the material world, come to be thought of as "tools," associated with but no longer an inseparable aspect of who we are. The body, we are often told, is corrupt, a hindrance, something to be endured. It is the arts and the martial arts, as well as Zen Buddhism in particular among the religions, however, that are best equipped to remind us of this deeper, natural state of being, and to help us return to that state through diligent practice. Thus, practice can be viewed as the process by which we come to know who we really are.

Unification of Body and Mind

In Japan, it is not that the typical man or woman on the street does not think of mind and body as separate and distinct, just as we in the West tend to do, but that beneath this "commonsense" belief is a long-standing tradition that the goal of living, and of discipline and practice, is to "reunite" what was already united at birth but was separated in the process of growing-up. In point of fact, mind/body unity has never been "severed," else our digestive system would not function, and we would be unable to coordinate our limbs. But when the need to learn a new skill arises, we do not know how to act in a unified manner. For example, to learn to play a musical instrument demands practice, with the hope that eventually what we think or imagine is exactly what we can play. When this is achieved it reveals that unity, at least within the traditions of the ways in Japan. You come to discover your deeper self, its spontaneous abilities and its connection to the greater cosmos.

Mind-body oneness is evident in the act of a tiny infant grasping an adult finger with surprising strength and able to fling the attached hand and arm of the adult from side to side in the crib with seeming ease. Without thinking, without deliberating, the tiny infant achieves remarkable strength spontaneously. Of course, the ultimate aim of the practice of self-cultivation (*shugyō*) is not to become children once more, but to become childlike as an achievement of intense training which leads one to the wisdom which infants and wild animals display spontaneously. It is a regained effortlessness and spontaneity of movement resulting in remarkable swiftness and power, which can only come at the end of discipline, at the middle or end of one's life, when one's diligence and awareness operate from a state of being which has achieved both integration and wisdom.

The nature of so-called mind-body unification or oneness needs to be further explained because it is not just associated with speed and strength. The *aikidō* master Tohei Koichi writes that mind-body unity means that "the body moves in accordance with the dictates of the mind and that the mind expresses itself through the body. The two are inseparable" (Tohei 2001b, 17). However, this crisp statement does not itself reveal the complexity involved in getting to that state where the body does as the mind dictates. It is Yuasa Yasuo who breaks new ground in dealing with the precise role that practice plays in this achievement. Thomas P. Kasulis, in his introduction to Yuasa's *The Body*, writes that mind-body unity is a state achieved only after years of spiritual and physical cultivation: it is "an achieved body-mind unity" (Yuasa 1987, 3). Such unity is not the normal or universal human condition, but rather it is an advanced state. Somehow, an opening, a pathway, a doorway has to be formed to allow passage between the conscious and the unconscious. Various breathing techniques seem to create such a pathway by taking over conscious control of an activity which is normally the work of the autonomic nervous system. This connection allows incredibly rapid response because there is no separation to overcome or to distract you from single-minded focus. Furthermore, such rapidity and spontaneity is enhanced by the unconscious mind taking control, as the conscious mind relinquishes control, yet remains fully aware. The years of practice allow you to act without thinking, without the slightest deliberation. Both the conscious and unconscious minds each benefit from this fuller harmony and integration. In fact, any of the Japanese Ways can bring about the opening of a pathway between the conscious and the unconscious, thereby allowing the body to respond with incredible rapidity to any challenge or situation. A swordsman in battle has no time to think of alternative paths to victory. To do so would mean death, for deliberation would create an "opening" for one's opponent, an interrupted response inviting an instantaneous strike by the opponent's sword. The response has to be instantaneous, purely responsive. The highly trained bodymind responds without the slightest thought or deliberation.

At first, the training of the body is awkward, and it seems uncooperative because consciousness is still in control, and we try to figure out how to hold our hands, our feet, when to inhale and exhale, and what to do about our rambling thoughts. But gradually there develops an "acquired naturalness," consciousness fades into the background of practice, and the body moves unconsciously without thinking or deliberation, able to respond to any situation in the flash of a sword. Only then will one discover the incredible power and wisdom which such unification yields. Tohei Koichi reminds us that "people often display powers in time of crisis that they would never dream of in ordinary life. Women have been known to lift automobiles to drag injured children out from under them" (Tohei 2001b, 18). These are spectacular once-only examples of mind-body unification, but they represent that of which we are capable.

Enlightenment

By training our breathing and our body we may achieve effortless movement and mind-body unity, but to what end? The increasing unification of mind and body achieved through the practice of controlling the breath and the moving of the body not only leads to great physical skills, it also leads to an experience of the unification of the individual with the greater whole. Mind-body unity is generalized to include an awareness of the oneness of self and other, and of self and universe. This is the Japanese understanding of enlightenment. Enlightenment is the direct experience of oneness with all that exists, and such a state of being is one in which one seems to become one with the flower, the rocks in a landscape garden, or the sorrows and suffering of others. With the expansion of power and the quickening of one's reflexes also comes the sensitization of the practitioner, resulting in the capacity for heartfelt identification with the wonders of existence itself. For the first time, one is truly at home in the universe. To be enlightened is to experience the world as a heartache, one is so in love with and so identified with whatever one beholds. As Dr. Sen Genshitsu (Soshitsu XV), a Grandmaster of the Way of Tea, expressed it, "there is now such joy in the moment, and you become so impressed by everything around you, that you could die!" The feelings are so intense, so enveloping: but the result is a heartache, and not a headache.

Living better and more mindfully as an increasingly harmonious and integrated bodymind is no small achievement. As exponents of Sōtō Zen[1] argue, every moment is an enlightened moment for one who has set out on a path, a way, and so rather than waiting for a blinding and perhaps isolated epiphany, every moment, every now, every flower, scent, and breeze becomes an epiphany, even if on a smaller scale. One's perception of self and

---

1. There are three major schools of Zen Buddhism in Japan, two of which are dominant: Rinzai Zen and Sōtō Zen. Briefly, the Rinzai school emphasizes sudden enlightenment and underscores the indispensability of an enlightenment experience. Such experiences are clearly set apart from ordinary experiences. The Sōtō school deemphasizes the importance of the blinding epiphany of enlightenment and instead sees enlightenment as practice. To decide to follow a path is itself enlightenment, and in that context every moment and every experience is an enlightenment experience. This is the gradual enlightenment position.

world have been remarkably altered, and continued practice will both sustain that transformation and open the door to further developments. Self-transformation is the meaning-content of self-cultivation. To achieve excellence, to become what you are capable of becoming in and from your depths, is what self-cultivation and self-transformation seek. Cultivation means a development in personality, and it is from this that the strongest ethical insights arise. To see the "other," whether human or not, whether sentient or not, as a source of wonder and delight, of worth and as a potential friend, is a profound foundation for thinking and acting ethically. It is a way-of-being-in-the-world which seeks to preserve and nurture, to embrace and assist whenever appropriate. It is a reverence for all that exists.

One of the central insights of practice is the folly of egoism and the recognition of the many delusions which result from concern for one's ego. It was the Buddha who taught that we will come to see the world as it really is through a practice which leads to a state of non-ego. Of course, Buddhist practice includes following the precepts and ethical norms for daily living, such as refraining from killing, stealing, lying, adultery, and the consumption of intoxicants, but the source of them all is the original insight of enlightenment. While the notion of cultivation is closely tied to Buddhism, its adaptation by the Japanese affected many aspects of their culture. Many of the artistic practices of Japan are methodologies of cultivation. Indeed, it would seem that any artistic practice taken in the broad sense can be viewed as a self-cultivational practice leading to enlightenment, for those with the dedication to pursue a practice with such diligence and seriousness of purpose. While the phrase "leading to enlightenment" should be taken to mean that it is enlightenment that is sought, enlightenment is to be found directly in the practice itself. Writing poetry mindfully, or being thrown by a partner in *aikidō*, is precisely where enlightenment is to be discovered. As a model of human living, the various practices can be taken to provide a general methodology for the living of all aspects of one's life: each and every moment can be as rich and magnificent as celebrating Tea, or the momentary snapshot of the "now" in haiku, or the vigilance and centeredness of *aikidō*.

Most importantly, the insights and personal development achieved through a practice are not meant to apply exclusively to the particular art through which they were learned but to one's life as a whole, by extension. One's whole bodymind is transformed by the specific practice, and one now walks and acts in the world differently. One will never see the world the way it was, for flowers are now more fragrant and exquisite than before, the bubbling of the boiling kettle in the tea room sounds like a remarkable symphony of nature, and one's "opponent" in *aikidō* has become a "partner" in mutual self-transformation. Each of these changes echoes throughout one's life experiences, changing whatever one sees, whatever one does, whatever one feels, like a shout bouncing off mountain peak after mountain peak, undoing the old rigidity and ushering in a new fluidity. To begin to see differently is to begin to act differently and to be different.

Meditation as a Path

Although not normally categorized as a "Way," meditation provides a path to enlightenment and is almost always an essential ingredient in all of the other paths. Meditation can take the form of repetitive practice in the martial arts, or intense focus on precise movement in making tea, arranging flowers, or making pottery, or talking to the rocks and plants as one constructs a landscape garden. Self-cultivation through meditation "is a method of training that strengthens and enhances the function of the mind to a higher level than the ordinary state . . . and strengthen[s] the power which synthesizes the functions of consciousness and the unconscious, while learning to control the emotional patterns (the habits of the mind/heart) [and other] complexes [which are] characteristic of oneself, with the view to further transform the mind" (Yuasa 1993,19). Meditation is, therefore, a component of self-cultivation. One who becomes increasingly self-integrated emotionally is more likely "to become a person who can relate . . . to another with love and in calmness" (Yuasa 1993, 20). It can be argued, therefore, that meditation enhances bodymind oneness and harmonizes conscious and unconscious functions, and in doing so actually paves the way to ethical behavior.

Emotional integration and a loving and empathetic attitude toward others goes a long way toward relational enhancement. Meditation helps to move one toward this kind of maturity as a person. And meditation is not only practiced in the customary sitting position that uses the body and its posture to control and expand the potential of the mind, but there is also a "meditation in motion," or walking meditation, which overtly utilizes the body-in-motion. Moreover, the many activities and skills of the various arts in Japan are themselves forms of meditation. Learning to hold the ladle just right in serving tea is a form of meditation, as is learning a specific move in *aikidō*, or deftly arranging a vase of flowers in one's home.

The Resultant Transformation

One of the most interesting comparisons made by Yuasa is the significance of personal cultivation in Japan and participation in sports generally. Western-style exercises and sports do not emphasize, or even include, breath focus and meditation, control of the emotions, or advancement toward *satori*. Yuasa offers a summary of his comparison:

> It would not be an exaggeration to say that, fundamentally, modern Western sports aim at competition in a game, or at winning over others in a match. This is true in all competitive games, and for this reason, the record becomes important. Also, competition arouses thrill and excitement in the viewers, from which is generated the idea of sports as a show, and we are now in the golden age of professional sports. Today, sports such as Olympic skiing and marathons have come to share a large market as a means for making money.
>
> By way of contrast, the standpoint of the performer or competitor has been valued as most important in Japanese artistry and the *bushi* way. . . . The goal of Japanese artistry and the *bushi* way is for the competitor or performer to discipline one's spirit by using one's body. And by transforming one's mind, a flower blossoms, whereby one achieves the state of "no-mind." The self ascends to the height at which it is no longer one's self, but is the self which harmonizes and accommodates others; it becomes one with the world and with the universe. (Yuasa 1993, 34–35)

Once more Yuasa hints at the ethical significance of cultivation when he asks, "isn't the most truly important thing for human beings the act of enhancing one's own mind and heart, while nurturing the soul which harmonizes with others?" (Yuasa 1993, 36).

Rather than asking what the relationship between mind and body is, "Eastern mind/body theory takes the attitude of asking how the mind-body relationship *becomes* or *changes* through training and practice" (Yuasa 1993, 62), with a view to comprehending the deeper or "original" state of being human. Theory and practice are inseparable, as are mind and body. To train the body is to train the mind, and, as will be seen particularly clearly in *aikidō*, to train the mind is also to train the body. There is only bodymind.

Ki

Ki is the Japanese translation of the Chinese *qi* (energy, spirit), as in *Qigong*. Yuasa tells us that in order to make clear the Japanese understanding of being-human-in-the-world, it is necessary to discuss *ki* energy (Yuasa 1993, 70). According to practitioners of the martial arts, the ultimate secret is the unification of body, mind, and *ki*. *Ki* can be thought of as an energy that flows through the body (and through the entire universe), and it is referred to as "mind" and is centered specifically in the lower abdomen (*seika tanden*). Paying attention to and developing the *tanden* (also referred to as the "ocean of *ki*") is fundamental to the martial arts, according to many practitioners. It is not unimportant that this area, just two or three inches below the navel, is referred to as "mind" or "consciousness." It points to a central aim and capacity in the martial arts; the unification of mind and *ki*. The flow of *ki* cannot be apprehended empirically, although meditation training can make one sensitive to the ebb and flow of *ki* as it courses through the network of meridians of the body. Eastern medicine is based on this meridian system, and whether it is acupuncture, acupressure, traditional herbal medicine, or *kiatsu*, they all base their practice on unblocking or regulating the flow of *ki* in the body and/or balancing that flow in the patient. *Ki*, the body, and the mind are one thing: the access point is through the body.

A Brief Map

In the chapters that follow, it will become evident that each and every one of the *dō* is a "moving meditative" path, the experience of which can be enlightenment, *satori* (also known as *kenshō*, the seeing into one's own nature). While Zen Buddhism is often thought to be the straightest path to *satori*, it is not the only one, nor is it for everyone the most efficient. Of course, enlightenment is an end which is not an end, since what one discovers in enlightenment is just how far there is still to grow, and that to continuously pursue a practice is itself enlightenment. "The Buddha is only half-way there," is a familiar quotation in Japan, even amongst non-Buddhists. The point of the saying is that even the Buddha is still on the path, still self-cultivating, still improving.

There simply is no final end, only the endless path with insights of profound significance along the way, each of which is an aspect of being enlightened. Even then, one still has to put what one has learned into everyday practice. To be able to put into practice what one thinks or knows is to apply one's insights and understanding to the moment-by-moment decisions of everyday living on an ongoing basis. To know that one is inextricably a part of the entirety of existence is not necessarily to act as though one were, or to see the same worth in another. To see another person as one's spiritual brother or sister is not necessarily to treat them well, as the history of siblings dating back to Cain and Abel will testify. To know how to make tea in the sunshine, when conditions are perfect, and one has the protection and seclusion of the tea hut or the Zen monastery, is one thing. But to be able to make tea properly when conditions are less than ideal and not at all as planned, when the guests or members of the audience are disinterested, already holding grudges against each other, grieved by an illness or a death, financially overwhelmed, and all of this taking place in a noisy gymnasium for purposes of demonstration, requires a master who is able to rise above the difficulties and the conflicts to create an atmosphere where the tea spirit is as evident as ever. Real life is unpredictable, complex, and unexpectedly difficult at times, and it is then that real mastery can become apparent: many can make tea in the sunshine, but it takes an accomplished master to make tea when it rains, when the unforseen threatens to disrupt one's anticipations and one's plans. It takes practice, deep concentration, a centered and imperturbable demeanor, a remarkable flexibility, and a steadfast sense of humor. Mastering the living of one's life, particularly in one's relationships with others, is no less demanding and, at times, seemingly overwhelming. The living of one's life is a never ending journey through self-cultivation, understanding, and steadfast compassion. Hopefully, there will come a time when one will be able to live honorably and compassionately even in the worst of storms. A true master can act on all occasions with grace, beauty, and compassion, even when it rains.

CHAPTER TWO

Aikidō—The Way of Peace

What is difficult to convey to someone who has not experienced the amazing environment that *aikidō*[1] creates is how remarkably transformative it is. Most come to *aikidō* from a sports background. *Aikidō* eliminates most competitiveness, teaches the importance of positive rather than negative thinking, creates a cheerful outlook, and turns physical contact into an act of friendship and the expression of goodwill. Whether or not one comes from a religious background, the flavor of genuine spirituality is here abundant: it does not replace religion but deepens it and renders the spiritual an actual, living, and direct experience. Ethically, one is taught how to show genuine respect for others and to make their learning and development one's own responsibility. The path, if steadfastly followed, leads directly to self-development, and the resultant self-development reveals that each of us is not only connected to the "other" but that we are connected to the entire universe. It is a "declaration of interdependence," a recognition that we are all manifestations of the creative force of the universe itself. Realizing this vast interconnection, and utilizing the resultant increase in power appropriately, is the basic aim of *aikidō*.

Aikidō is a term consisting of three elements or meanings: *ai* means harmony, *ki* means energy, and *dō* means way. *Aikidō* is the pathway which leads to the harmony of *ki* energy: it leads

---

1. There are a number of different styles or "schools" of *aikidō*, each with its own particular emphasis. In this chapter I will focus on the original Aikikai tradition of Ueshiba Morihei (the founder of *aikidō*) and his son and successor, Kisshōmaru, as well as on the teachings of Tohei Koichi, the founder of the Ki Society.

21

one to a harmony of body and mind, a harmony with all that exists in this world of form, including one's adversaries, and of an individual with the universe, or universal.

The Beginnings

As part of my research grant, which enabled me to meet with many of the grand masters of the various "Ways," I was invited to attend the World Camp of *aikidō*, in Utsunomiya, in Tochigi Prefecture, about an hour and a half northwest of Tokyo. The camp takes place at the headquarters and also the home of Tohei-sensei. Over the next seven days, I was to encounter several dozen of the most outstanding *aikidōka*s in the world. The skill level was extraordinary, and the immense and beautiful *dōjō* was seven hundred mats in size, said to be the largest *dōjō* in the world. Together with meeting halls, housing for a large number, an excellent dining room, two full Japanese-style baths, one each for men and women, and beautiful landscaping, the headquarters itself inspires a sense of community. The importance of a friendly atmosphere was apparent from the beginning, as all participants were warmly welcomed and helpfully settled. An air of good cheer and of being wholeheartedly welcomed was a central quality of both staff and participants. Such attitudes are, in fact, central to the teachings of Tohei Koichi's Ki Society. To be less than positive and welcoming is to weaken one's own *ki* and dampen everyone else's, just as a positive outlook can uplift others. Clearly there was something special about the atmosphere of the place, where each participant, stranger or not, immediately sensed becoming an integral part of the group.

Throughout, there was a constant reminder, both in photographs reverently bowed to and in communication, that the creator of *aikidō*, Ueshiba Morihei, or O-sensei (great or honored teacher),[2] was the founder of this incredible practice as a way of self-cultivation. What is important about O-sensei is that he distilled the most important aspects of the many martial arts which he studied into a new form that yielded such power that he became, in the eyes of a great many, the most skilled martial

---

2. The reader should note that Ueshiba Morihei, the founder of *aikidō*, will sometimes be referred to as O-sensei, or as Ueshiba-sensei.

artist alive. His new martial art form eventually attracted a sizeable following of students and is now to be found in most of the countries of the world. What he taught was not just a series of moves, but an intangible spirituality which was contagious, yet its precise nature was not evident either to him or to his students. It was his remarkable student, Tohei Koichi, who later came to work out in detail what this intangible something was that O-sensei manifested and represented. Tohei Koichi made the spiritual methodologically clear and accessible.

O-sensei (1883–1969) was sent to a Buddhist temple near his home in Tanabe, Wakayama Prefecture, to study the Confucian classical writings and Buddhist scripture. His father taught him sumo wrestling and swimming, in part because he was such a small and weak child. Later, he moved to Tokyo, establishing his own stationary store, but more importantly, he began studying *aikijujutsu* and swordsmanship of the Shinkage tradition. An illness forced him to abandon his store, which he gave to his employees, and return home to convalesce. In 1904, he volunteered to serve in the Russo-Japanese war, but was rejected because he was under five feet in height. Gleason remarks that this rejection "infuriated him. Eager to serve his country, he trained vigorously, alone in the mountains, and even hung for long periods of time by his arms from tree branches, hoping to stretch his height" (Gleason 1995, 8). The next time he applied, he was accepted. He served with honor, supposedly performing both heroic and remarkable feats of bravery. After he returned home from the war, his father engaged the *judōka* Takagi Kiyochi, who was then visiting Tanabe, to act as Morihei's teacher, and converted the family barn into a *dōjō* (Ueshiba 1991, 9). He also continued to study swordsmanship.

In 1910 the government announced an incentive plan to entice people to journey to unsettled land in the north, and in 1912 Morehei's small family and more than eighty other people from his district left for the then isolated northern island of Hokkaido. With O-sensei as leader of the group, they chose to settle at Shiratake, which was then "a wasteland, and the colonists had to struggle against appalling weather and poor soil conditions to bring it under cultivation" (Ueshiba 1991, 9). Cultivate it they did, however, and the community succeeded in growing crops, raising horses, husbanding cattle, and in building a small lumber industry. They also established a primary school. In Hokkaido, O-sensei met Takeda Sokaku, who taught Daito Ryu *aikijujutsu*. Shiratake, at the height of its success, was destroyed by fire in 1917. The community rebuilt, but in 1919, upon hearing of his father's serious illness, Ueshiba, along with his family, chose to return to Tanabe after nearly eight years in the Hokkaido wilderness. His journey back to Tanabe was interrupted by a visit with the charismatic head of a new Shintō sect (Ōmoto-kyo), Deguchi Ōnisaburō, whom he thought might be able to heal his father. But his father passed on before he reached his bedside and, after a period of grieving, O-sensei moved to Ayabe to be with Ōnisaburō, with whom he worked for the next eight years. He established a *dōjō* of his own, first for followers of Ōmoto-kyo and then for many others, as "word began to spread that there was an exceptional master of the martial arts living in Ayabe" (Ueshiba 1991, 11). It was here that he began to develop his own style of martial art, combining the several traditions which he had studied, but also adding insights of his own. He called it *aikibujutsu*.

In 1924, Ueshiba and Ōnisaburō decided to journey to Mongolia and Manchuria, "in search of a holy land where they could establish a new world government based on religious precepts" (Ueshiba 1991, 12). It was in Mongolia where O-sensei's earliest indication of paranormal ability became evident: "he could see flashes of light indicating the path of oncoming bullets. The discovery of this intuitive sense was a profound experience for Morihei and, after returning to Japan, he frequently encountered situations where he felt manifestations of a spiritual force" (Ueshiba 1996, 13). In 1925 he engaged a master of the Way of the Sword, *kendō*, and defeated him without actually fighting "because he could sense the direction in which the blows would fall before the officer's wooden sword could strike him" (Ueshiba 1991, 13–14). It was immediately after this that he had his first religious experience:

> All of a sudden I felt like the sky was descending. From out of the earth, golden energy was spouting forth like a fountain. That warm energy encircled me and my body and mind became very light and clear. I could even understand the murmurings of the small birds around me.

At that moment I could understand that my life's work in *budō* was actually based on divine love and the laws of creation. I was unable to stop my tears and I wept freely. Since that time I've known that this great earth itself is my house and home. The sun, moon, and stars each belong to me. Since that time I've never felt any attachment to property or possessions. (Gleason 1995, 16–17)

The experience of merging with the universe serves as the foundation of the philosophy of *aikidō*. With it comes the recognition that the martial arts are never about attack, but always about defense and the defusing of aggression. This martial art teaches the centrality of love and mutual growth and development. *Aikidō* is a method of merging with the spirit of the universe, and this idea can be traced back to Shintō, Buddhism, and Zen Buddhism. In the same year, Ueshiba-sensei had another remarkable experience in which he came to realize "that the deepest enlightenment of *budō* is one with that of religion and tears of ecstacy flowed freely" (Gleason 1995, 18).

The *aikidō* path of self-cultivation is one of achieving body-mind unity, unity with the "universal," and always unity with one's partners in practice, to be carried out of and beyond the *dōjō* into everyday life. "*Aikidō* is the way of nonresistance and is therefore undefeatable from the start. . . . Merely by having the intention to fight with one who embodies the universal law, they have fixed their mind on violating the harmony of nature itself" (Gleason 1995, 19). What is demanded of us in our personal growth and development is coming to grasp the laws and order of the universe and our relationship to it, and accepting "the responsibility for the well-being of this planet and all life upon it" (Gleason 1995, 22).

This idea of all things emanating from or being a self-manifestation of the universal source is as old as Daoism and as recent as the influential philosophy of Nishida Kitarō (1870–1945). In Daoism, the invisible, formless, thingless, originating energy, as the Dao that cannot be spoken of, gave birth to the Dao which can be spoken of. It can be spoken of as the *yin* and the *yang* of creation, the two complementary forces which are the engines of production, growth, change, decay, and motion. From these two come the "ten-thousand things," or all existence as form.

More recently, Nishida remarked that "the universe is not a creation of God but a manifestation of God" (Nishida 1990, 158). As such, it can be said of each consciousness that it "is one part of God's consciousness and its unity comes from God's unity" (Nishida 1990, 161). And insofar as each of us is "divine" in our origin, the easiest pathway to a direct experience of God, or divinity, or the universal is an inward one:

> An infinite power is hidden even in our small chests that are restricted by time and space; the infinite unifying power of reality is latent in us. Possessing this power, we can search for the truth of the universe in learning, we can express the true meaning of reality in art, and we can know the foundation of reality that forms the universe in the depths of our hearts—we can grasp the true face of God. The infinitely free activity of the human heart proves God directly. As Jakob Boehme said, we see God with a "reversed eye" (*umgewandt Auge*). (Nishida 1990, 81)

By a "reversed eye" is meant the act of introspecting, of looking within rather than without. One's focus of attention is redirected from the external world, to the internal world of consciousness itself. The "divine" is deep within, at that empty place where knower and known, God and self are experienced as one and the same.

In describing mind and body unity, Tohei[3] begins by noting that we received from the universe "two elements, the body and the spirit" (Tohei 1966, 21). And the relationship between these two consists in the body moving in accordance with the dictates of the spirit or mind and the mind or spirit using the body. "The continuation of human life is impossible with only one of the two, but when they join together we are able to manifest our highest abilities and our innate powers" (Tohei 1966, 21). His son, Tohei Shinichi, whom I had the good fortune to interview, added that the unification of mind and body is the natural state at birth: they are originally one. As it is the natural state, it is the

---

3. The reader will understand that in referring to a revered teacher, one would always add "sensei" as an expression of respect. I will omit it in order to make reading less repetitive.

easiest and most effortless state. The regaining of this natural state is to be achieved through the continued practice of *aikidō*, and the lessons and insights gained are to be applied to our everyday lives. It is incumbent on us to practice *aikidō* in everything we do or say. It is a twenty-four-hour-a-day engagement. The elder Tohei was too ill to meet with me during the World Camp, but in anticipatory conversations with those who had arranged for my visit, he emphasized that if it was technique I was interested in talking about, then he was not interested. Of course, it was not technique that I was interested in, but the underlying philosophy of *aikidō*, and ethics. His son served as an able and insightful alternative and, on occasion, intermediary. He stressed that his father does not use the term "enlightenment," just "oneness with the universe." "The problem with 'enlightenment' is that often its usage does not include the universe in its frame of reference, but only the self. Becoming one with the universe is not a matter of self-enhancement, but requires a forgetting of the self. Furthermore, enlightenment can easily be thought of as a thing, or a possession, and then the mind stops."

Aikidō: One and Not One

Aikidō is not a unified tradition, although all schools and traditions trace their beginnings to the founder, Ueshiba Morihei. The major "split" occurred in 1974, when Tohei Koichi, the only "tenth dan" at the time and the chief instructor worldwide as appointed by Ueshiba-sensei (indeed, he was chosen as the person to bring *aikidō* to the West, and he did so beginning in 1953, in Hawaii), broke away from the Aikikai, the original school, which was headed by O-sensei's son, Ueshiba Kisshōmaru, and formed the Ki Society. As early as 1971, Tohei-sensei began teaching *ki* classes outside the walls of the Aikikai, because his teaching of *ki* was thought to be a deviation from the more technical teachings and practice. Regarding the split, Stone and Meyer summarize George Simcox's analysis: "The big difference . . . is that mainstream *aikidō* proceeds from the premise that continuous, rigorous physical practice will lead in time to the *aiki* attitude. This *aiki* attitude is described as a relaxed/centered approach to attacks on the mat and the conflicts of life in general. The Ki Society's goal, from day one, is to train the *aiki* attitude. They call it *Ki* training" (Stone and Meyer 1995, 171).

No doubt there were many reasons for the split, but reflecting back, Tohei-sensei recounts the need for freedom and the space to teach *aikidō* in a way that was less shrouded in the mysteries of Shintō and more accessible to anyone who wished to learn *aikidō*'s principles and practice them. But that first required extracting those principles and formulating them in a manner that would allow anyone to teach them. The genius of Ueshiba-sensei is unquestioned by any who ever had contact with him. He was the living embodiment of *aikidō* at its best, and his skills were so finely honed that no one else was able to achieve his heights. Many say it was Tohei who came the closest. Tohei was the pedagogical genius of *aikidō*, the one who systematized *aikidō* as something communicable to anyone, and who developed the testing procedures for assessing bodymind unification. A contemporary American instructor of *aikidō*, Rod Kobayashi, states that:

> He was the one who developed a method of training. The Founder of *aikidō*, Master Ueshiba, might have been the Founder, but to explain *aikidō*, I think nobody can outdo Master Tohei. You just can't beat the way that he explains the principles and the practice of *aikidō*. He really understood and I think he really developed a method of training. The Founder's like an inventor . . . but it was Master Tohei who had to develop *aikidō*. (Stone and Meyer 1995, 157)

A similar view is expressed by Frank Doran, an instructor from Redwood City, California:

> Having been a teacher myself now for a considerable time, and experiencing a lot of good teachers, the thing that I always hone in on with Tohei-sensei is that he was a master teacher . . . he was a genius. I've listened to many . . . today who have said the same thing, that he was a genius as a teacher. So apparently, in his own language, he was quite something. It's important to note for Americans too, when he was speaking in English, that we were still captivated by his magnetism: his personal *ki* was very strong. (Stone and Meyer 1995, 141)

Tohei himself claims that his understanding of *aikidō* is thirty percent Ueshiba-sensei and seventy percent his own (Tohei 1996a, 13). And while O-sensei was such a major force in his development, he speaks of two other teachers of importance. Ogura Tetsuju taught him *misogi* (a purificatory practice), "which involved chanting at full voice from morning to night, throughout which the senior students would strike your back strongly without reserve" (Tohei 2001a, 115). It was at a time when Tohei was very seriously ill as a result of a chest injury incurred in *judō* practice, which developed into pleurisy. Health did not return, and Tohei decided to throw himself into *misogi*. Judged too ill to withstand the rigors of *misogi*, Ogura sent him off to do Zen meditation (*zazen*). Zealous in his *zazen* training, after six months he was allowed to begin *misogi* practice. Not yet fully recovered, his chest began to cause him pain once more due to the demands of *misogi*, but he was steadfastly determined to see it through. At the end of a three-day session, his pleurisy had completely disappeared. The lesson which he took from Ogura and *misogi* was "that if we turn and face our difficulties we find that they vanish" (Tohei 2001a, 116).

From O-sensei Tohei learned how to relax completely. O-sensei taught his students "to do sharp, powerful techniques," and yet he himself was totally relaxed: "what Sensei said and what he did were two different things" (Tohei 1996a, 13). This became crystal clear to Tohei when he journeyed to Hawaii to instruct. Hawaiians are, as a rule, tall and strong, and many of the techniques taught by O-sensei simply did not work. Tohei had to rethink *aikidō* because of this physical difference, and central in this was the realization that it was not a matter of strength or muscle power, but of total relaxation, which ensured that he was centered in his one point, *seika tanden* or *hara*, the locus of *ki*.

The third major influence was Nakamura Tenpu, from whom he learned that "the mind moves the body." He writes that after learning this, "I watched Ueshiba-sensei perform *Aikidō* arts, [and] it was clear that he was leading the opponent's mind, and therefore able to lead his body. He could do this because the mind leads the body" (Tohei 2001a, 118). Working this through, he concluded that "before you can lead your opponent's mind or direct his *Ki*, you must first be able to control your own mind and *Ki*. In other words, before you can win over an opponent you must first win over yourself," which means that the unification of mind and body must be present "just as we receive them together from the universe" (Tohei 2001a, 118).

Aikidō and *Budō*

Given that the mind must lead the body and that one's own mind must be under control, it is imperative that the mind not allow itself to be distracted by focusing on an arm movement, or the flash of a blade, or the touch on one's body. Similarly, a fear as to whether one is likely to be able to successfully complete whatever it is that one has set out to do also serves to distract and stop the mind at a time when it should be alert to any threat. Furthermore, not only will a distracted mind stop itself, but negative thinking will also do so. Negative thinking stops the mind, as, for example when one focuses on failure, or on one's own lack of ability, or on the frightening quality of one's adversary. One will never know what one is capable of if one undermines the possibility of success by dwelling on failure. Instead, imagine positively that you will do your best. This frees the mind to survey the situation and to select the best course of action for whatever it is that emerges from the unknown that one is about to encounter. In *aikidō*, the mind leads the body and, in doing so, the two are in harmony, are as one. For example, when deciding to cross a busy street by jaywalking, it is a serious mistake to be indecisive in the midst of executing the decision to cross where and when one is not supposed to cross. To be fearful or divided in the midst of crossing the street is a formula for serious injury. The mind will hold you back, for you did not first unify mind and body, and it will continue to send you warnings, which will translate as hesitation and indecisiveness. But if you unify mind and body, and it is your decision to cross, then it is because you "know" you can make it if you are focused on the traffic and its speed, the distance to travel, the condition of the road, and any other factors which emerge as you begin your dash. Your mind is focused but not fixated, allowing you to scan as you run, to revise as you execute your plan, thereby enabling you to deal with the unforeseen and with miscalculations. The moving mind that is focused but not fixated was a *key* teaching of the Yagyū school of swordsmanship, in which O-sensei earned a teaching

certificate during his early years of study and practice. He would
have been aware of the teachings of Takuan Sōhō (1573–1645),
a Zen priest and abbot of Daitoku-ji temple, in Kyoto, who
served as a teacher to Japan's most famous samurai, Musashi Miyamoto, as well as a consultant to Yagyū Munenori
(1571–1646), who was the head of the Yagyū Shinkage school of
swordsmanship. Takuan taught that one should act from one's
unconscious, from *mushin* or one's no-mind. The mind must
never be stopped, but must be ever relaxed yet alert, able to take
in the widest field of consciousness and able to move from focus
to focus as necessary without losing the awareness of the whole.
An agile, moving mind is able to take in both figure and ground,
both background and foreground, both focus and periphery, and
because of this is never surprised. A mind that does not fixate
is never caught off guard: it never presents an opening for an
attacker. Tohei Shinichi remarked that the universal itself is best
thought of as a verb: it is not a steady state, for it never stops, it
is limitless, and it is always exemplified by change. A Buddhist
might say that the Buddha is impermanence, so in *aikidō* reality
as the universal is constant movement, and yet it remains so calm
that we can feel our connection with the entire cosmos. This is
Takuan's "immoveable wisdom" (*fudochi shinmyo ryoku*), and
like the statue of Kwannon, the goddess of mercy who is por-
trayed as having a thousand arms, one is able to attend and to
act in any and all directions, for one has not been "captured" by
any one action, emotion, or thought. It is an immoveable moving
that one does, or an imperturbable fluidity. The mind must remain unattached, so that the body can move freely. Gleason describes this state as moving with one's "whole body and mind, at
one with both movement and rest. It is to move with complete
stability and centeredness, in harmony with our partner and unattached to the success of our technique" (Gleason 1995, 15).

A Spiritual Way

It should be evident by now that *aikidō* is not a martial art in the
sense that it is about fighting spirit, or the mastering of technique as
an end in itself. Its focus is on self-cultivation, and the key to self-
cultivation is the development of mind-body harmony and an increase in *ki* energy, as both of these contribute to the insight that

each of us is already one with the universal.[4] Finding the power in ourselves which *ki* represents reminds us that this surprising power is at least akin to the power of the universe as creator and sustainer of all that is. *Aikidō* seeks to achieve enlightenment or *satori*, in Zen terms. And the main road or pathway to such realization, in virtually all of the traditions known, is breath or breathing. When I interviewed the legendary Suzuki Shinichi, in Maui, I asked what the one thing was that he would like to share with me that was the most important, the most essential aspect of his lifetime as an *aikidōka* and *aikidō* master. He replied without hesitation, "nothing is more important than breathing, breathing, breathing." He urged me to do *aikidō* breathing every day for at least fifteen minutes and preferably for thirty minutes. Controlled breathing unifies the conscious and unconscious aspects of mind, which seems central to enlightenment. In *aikidō* breathing one "must draw in the *ki* of the universe completely and concentrate it in the single spot in the lower abdomen. In other words, we feel as if we were drawing the universal into our own abdomen." With practice you will forget your body and your breathing which now simply happens, and you "will have entered a world of nothing but breathing. You will feel as if it is the universal, not you yourself, who is doing the breathing." Eventually, as you continue to practice breathing, "you will come to comprehend yourself as a part of the universal" (Tohei 1966, 28–30). *Aikidō* breathing is meditation, and *aikidō* on the tumbling mats is also "Zen in motion and it brings the reality of Zen to the surface" (Gleason 1995, 13). In addition to this statement by a longtime student of Zen Buddhism, Gleason also quotes D. T. Suzuki, who wrote that "the teaching and practice of Morihei Ueshiba is at one with that of Mahāyāna Buddhism, and also the way of Zen. . . . Although it is not based on any formal study of Zen Buddhism, Ueshiba-sensei's experience is definitely what is referred to in the Far East as *satori*" (Gleason 1995, 13).

While Tohei was greatly influenced by Zen, Gleason maintains that it is Shintō which supplies the spiritual roots of *aikidō*.

---

4. The "universal," "*Ki*," and "Nature," all refer to the ultimate source of all that exists. As Tohei Koichi writes, "If we ask where life came from before the creation of man we have no answer but that it came from the universal. If this is so, our own lives too proceed from the universal," as does everything else (Tohei 1966, 14). This ultimate source is a "state we call *Ki*. Many call it God; others call it Buddha, and still others by other names depending on where they live" (Tohei 1962, 23).

And given the fact that O-sensei devotedly practiced Shintō worship both at the shrine which he built on the grounds of his *dōjō* and by frequently adopting the cleansing ritual of *misogi*, dousing himself with ice-cold water regardless of the temperature or time of year, it is evidently so. *Kannagara no michi*, the stream of God or the flow of creative energy which is ever present in the universe, is the ancient pathway from which Shintō itself developed, explains Saotome. Shintō, or the way of the *kami*, like *kannagara*, "is a way of intuition. There are no written laws, no strict doctrines of right or wrong. The only laws are the laws which govern natural phenomena and promote harmony. *Kannagara* is a way of supreme freedom, for the action appropriate to function in harmony with nature occurs spontaneously" (Saotome 1993, 21). Saotome and others have detailed this aspect of O-sensei's background; it is unnecessary to repeat it here (Saotome 1993; Gleason 1995). What is important here is to suggest the likely results of Shintō influence on the ethical dimension of *aikidō*.

Aikidō and Ethics

Shintō's contribution to *aikidō* is to be found in its emphasis on character and attitude. While ethics is a social matter, Shintō insists that it is perfection of character that serves as the bedrock for proper interpersonal relationships. Shintō teaches how to be Japanese in the sense that the ways-of-behaving-well-in-the-world are to be found in its practice. Thus, it is not enough to chart the proper ways of behaving in social relationships; it is also important to perfect one's own character and attitudes, such as being cheerful, or being thankful for the privilege of existing in this wondrous world. These are aspects of character development, and while each aspect of one's character impacts one's social and, therefore, ethical relationships, the emphasis is not on the outside but on the inside. A good person, deeply settled in his or her character achievements, will act well in relation to others, including the "other" as the environment. The outside and inside are really one, of course, but the issue is how one prepares a human being to behave well in the outside world: the answer seems to be to create healthy and wholesome persons. To be wholeheartedly thankful for having been given the gift of existence will affect the way in which one works and plays in the world, both when alone and with others.

It has been said that "the conventional use of the word Shintō hides a baffling variety of rituals, beliefs, and community structures" (Teeuwen 1996, 37). Nonetheless, there are key beliefs and attitudes which seem to have been held more or less throughout the history and development of the Shintō tradition. Chief among these is the expression "the Way of the *kami*" (*kannagara no michi*), where *kami* refers to the awesome, or extraordinary, or the divine nature which appears throughout the natural universe. *Michi* means something like the sacred blood, energy, or spirit of the cosmos and is the cosmic vitalizing force or energy, "and may be taken to be the present biological link between individual man [and woman] and the cosmos, including the *Kami*" (Herbert 1967, 44). Jean Herbert claims that *michi* "is probably the most expressive term in the Japanese vocabulary of ethics and religion," for it can refer to a person of character or integrity, and it links "the subject in some awe-inspiring way with the height and depth of the great All" (Herbert 1967, 45). To be in tune with the *michi* of the *kami* is to flow with the All both effortlessly and spontaneously. It seems clear that *aikidō*'s emphasis on flowing with the *ki* of the universal, becoming one with it such that one flows effortlessly and spontaneously as circumstances present themselves to be dealt with, has much in common with this ancient Shintō perspective.

Another key teaching of Shintō is the importance of sincerity or integrity (*makoto*). *Makoto* is central in most of the traditions of the Far East; in Confucianism, Daoism, Chinese Buddhism, Zen Buddhism, and Shintō. Watsuji Tetsurō (1889–1960) held that *makoto* was the root of truthfulness, honesty, and trustworthiness, all of which are necessary for anything resembling dependable and worthwhile social interaction and, as such, it is the foundation of all human relationships (Watsuji 1996, 48).[5] It seems to imply that one who has *makoto* is honest and self-reflective, such that one is vigilant in facing one's shortcomings

---

5. Watsuji writes that "*makoto* implies . . . that one is pure and without falsehood in one's attitude of mind as well as in one's words and deeds." Watsuji also defines *makoto* as "the path of Heaven, 'sincerity,' and truthfulness." He writes, "human beings are obliged to fulfil the task of bringing deceitfulness to nought and of making truthfulness manifest." Truthfulness and deceit are both based on trust, in the sense that "to deceive another person is a betrayal of trust. It cannot occur at a place where there is no trust. Seen in this light, we can say that truthfulness is decided in and through the human relation that consists in a relationship of trust" (Watsuji 1996, 273–75).

and steadfast in working toward one's continuing character betterment. Sincerity demands complete commitment, a putting of heart, mind, soul, and body into whatever it is that one does. Such integrity inevitably results in benevolence, faithfulness, and loyalty. It is the fastidious attempt to keep oneself unsullied by selfish desire, hatred, ill will, or a shriveled sense of reality as purely material. It is *makoto* that leads to group harmony; it implies solidarity of community feeling which manifests itself as peacefulness, goodwill, and happiness or cheerfulness, and of a sense of thankfulness for one's existence and for any good that may befall one due to the acts of others.

With this background in mind, perhaps we might imagine ourselves entering an *aikidō dōjō*. The morning air is crisp, and you can already feel the energy which flows from the morning practice. As you enter, you bow as a sign of respect, just as when you leave the exercise mats at the end, you bow once more. Of course you remove your shoes, just as you would upon entering a Japanese home, so as not to track inside the dirt and grime of everyday life from the outer world. The *dōjō* is a place of purity, and purity and acts of purification are central to Shintō as well. One never enters a Shintō shrine without first having washed one's hands and rinsed out one's mouth. Whether shrine or *dōjō*, one is given the chance to renew oneself, to begin again as it were and to do things right. O-sensei writes almost lyrically about the *dōjō* which we are about to enter with a pure heart, an intensity which is considerable, and a sense of goodwill and cheerfulness which is contagious:

> My *dōjō* is nature; it is the universe. It is truly a dwelling, a *dōjō* and a temple built by Kami. If you look with the eyes of your heart, it is the teacher that possesses the scientific and spiritual truth which will lead you to enlightenment. It is all the sacred scriptures. The laws of nature have come into being through the function of love, the absolute harmony found in the unfolding process of creation. It is imperative that those on the path of *Aikidō* practice with these things held deep within their hearts. (Saotome 1993, 67)

You may recall being instructed that if you are not in a happy state of mind and eager to take part with full vigor, that you would be better not to come to the *dōjō*. *Aikidō* stresses over and over again that whatever one does one should do with a positive mind; a "plus mind rather than a minus mind" as Tohei reminds his students over and over again. One minus mind can unsettle an entire group of plus minds, destroying group harmony, just as one ill-willed or grumpy individual at a party can dash the party before it begins. Of course, one joyful and spirited individual can uplift a gathering, and turn something humdrum into something exciting and memorable. In *aikidō*, not only must the entering student have a positive mind, it is essential for the teacher as well: "whenever you enter the *dōjō* you must be in a positive frame of mind. Your students come to the *dōjō* in order to change their minds from minus to plus. If the instructor is minus, there is no need to come" (Reed 1992, 286).

You have yet to set foot on the exercise mats, but already you have shown respect, bowed with humility, and ensured that you are entering with a positive mind and a keen desire to learn with intensity. You step on the mats and, in doing so, you are now part of a plus-minded community of people who strive to live and practice in harmony. What struck me forcibly at World Camp in Japan was the incredible joy and goodwill that prevailed, even with a hundred or more involved. On one occasion, when the Japanese black belts joined those of us from the West who had been there for the full week, a young *aikidōka* rushed up to me and, with a beautiful smile on his face, asked in Japanese if he could be my partner. He was a black belt and I was something of an observer. "*Onegai shimasu!*" he said in a singsong cadence; "please, will you work out with me?" He wanted to teach me, and he wanted us to get to know each other, even if only in a small way. His enthusiasm was contagious! I can still see his smiling face, generously offering his services mostly for my benefit, although *aikidō* teaches that teaching is an essential aspect of learning *aikidō*. Not to teach what you have learned is not really to have learned it at all.

You bow to your sensei, stretch as you need to, and then line up in the sitting *seiza* position (feet folded under buttocks), waiting for the session to begin. There now is no talking, and there certainly is none when the sensei talks. All bow to the photos of the founder(s) at the front of the *dōjō*, then to the instructor, and the instructor to the students. There is a reading to remind one of the basic principles of *aikidō*, and then the practice begins, or, as sometimes is the case, there is breathing meditation. One increases one's *ki*, extends one's *ki* outward, and is now ready to begin the practice with even more energy available than before. Then comes the biggest surprise of all, or at least it was for me. The practice begins and there is usually throwing and tumbling involved. I have never before encountered people so eager to be thrown by another human being: "*onegai shimasu.*" Please throw me, and I will gladly throw you. It is not a matter of competition, or winning, or showing who has superior strength. It is a matter of personal development and engaging the other person as a partner who is willingly and actively involved in your personal development as well as her/his own. Women toss men, men toss women, and rather than aggression and ill will, there is laughter and looks of delight and sheer joy on the faces of those involved. I have seen long lines of people being thrown by those chosen to throw, one after another, and the looks on the faces remind one of the joys on the playground as a child. There is often laughter, as well as praise for a tumble well executed. This is not the typical athletic complex scene, and the distinction between *aikidō* and sport is a vital one, a theme which I shall expand shortly.

The Value and Worth of the Other

Aikidō is not simply the learning of technique, yet the way to learn what *aikidō* has to teach is through technique. O-sensei himself wrote that "ultimately, you must forget about technique. The further you progress, the fewer teachings there are. The Great Path is really No Path" (Ueshiba 1992, 114). This same thinking applies to ethics in Japan: one learns the rules early on but, as one matures as a person it is not the rules that keep one on the ethical path, it is the transformation that has taken place in your personality that now spontaneously responds to situations with a benevolent heart, a sense of identification with the joys and sorrows of others, a strong desire to help, and a clear vision of what those people could become. Ethics is a self-manifestation of who a person is and, at the more developed levels, there is no need for rules and regulations: one is spontaneously benevolent and other-directed simply because that is now who one is. One has become no-minded, no longer filled with ego and self-importance. A developmentally advanced human being understands that we are all manifestations of the same creative energy. O-sensei taught that "all people share the same divine origin. There is only one thing that is wrong or useless. That is the stubborn insistence that you are an individual, separate from others" (Gleason 1995, 6). By contrast, what one learns on the mats is that "*aikidō* is a path where one progressively encounters the true self with wonder and joy; the estranged self, hidden with its inexhaustible potential, lies undiscovered by many people who die without even knowing that it exists" (Gleason 1995, 32). Saotome states this in theological terms: "The truth of I AM is that I am the other. I am a part of God. I am a part of the cosmos. I am a part of the earth. I am part of you. I AM is [the] true God [of] Consciousness, Universal Ego" (Saotome 1993, 138). In an amusing exchange, O-sensei was asked by Saotome, "'How can you see God?' He pointed at himself and then at me. 'My God perceived your God'" (Saotome 1993, 152).

A major part of ethics is being able to recognize the value and worth of another. It is present, though sometimes totally obscured, even in the depths of a truly evil person. But even in such a person, the original mind, the divine origin is still present, waiting to be discovered, freed, and nourished. For many this never happens, but what this talk of original mind makes evident is that the Japanese do not view human beings as intrinsically evil and originally corrupted. This is the fundamental starting point of ethics in Japan, it seems to me. All education must be aimed at bringing out this innate goodness, this innate sense of right and wrong based on a human-heartedness. In a strikingly similar way, Plato referred to the inborn "knowledge" of goodness as "recollection," and he charted the pathway which could lead to a remembering of what it is that every person already has within but is as yet unable to see clearly or at all. All teaching is reminding, and were it not so it is difficult to comprehend how it could be taught in the first place. Unless you already know it, in some sense, how would you be able to recognize it were you to see it? One of the meanings of the Latin *educere* is to draw out. The other meaning is to put in, which tends to be the ordinary understanding of education. Drawing out presupposes that what is to be drawn out is already there, but somehow obscured. Ethical maturity is about coming to be who you already are.

O-sensei and *aikidō* extend this original goodness to apply to all things. Tohei writes that:

> Looking at something with the eyes of the spirit means viewing that thing from the viewpoint of its real essence. From the viewpoint of the real essence of the universal, all of us, the whole world, all humanity, are of the same womb with all trees, all grass, and everything to the clouds and the mists. Can a reason exist then for fighting or hatred? You will first be able to understand the *aikidō* spirit of loving and protecting all things, and the *aikidō* injunction against fighting if you look at the question from the viewpoint of the basic essence of the universal. (Tohei 1966, 88)

Aikidō and Sports

Many, if not most, view the martial arts as a cluster of aggressive sports. Movies portray martial artists as superhuman killing machines, and such films are rated "R" because of the "extreme violence" involved. Even the mild *Karate Kid* series depicts the "good" martial artist teacher as the exception, surrounded by heads of other schools as ego-filled, aggressive, and set upon winning at any cost. *Aikidō* is neither aggressive nor a sport.

The historical background to *aikidō* is *budō*, the Way of the Martial Arts. *Budō* represents an evolutionary history, meaning that its beginnings were, in fact, aggressive but came to be quite the opposite because of the influence of Zen Buddhism.[6] Saotome describes this change as "an evolution etched in blood" (Saotome 1993, 104). He describes *aikidō* as having "its roots in conflict, its seed sown deep in the rich spawning ground of Japanese soil and nourished with the blood of the warrior"

---

6. Nitobe Inazo writes that the literal translation of *Bu-shi-dō* is "Military-Knight-Ways—the ways which fighting nobles should observe in their daily life as well as in their vocations; in a word, the 'Precepts of Knighthood'" (Nitobe 1969, 4). It is an unwritten moral code for "a rough breed who made fighting their vocation." *Budō* refers to the martial ways, i.e., the various martial arts. *Bu* is often used in the same way, but it can more specifically refer to military skill, or one's capacity to handle weapons.

(Saotome 1993, 104). The image left is of a fierce fighter, sworn to defend his lord, whether right or wrong, to the death if need be. Each samurai warrior had to face death in every waking moment, in order to be steeled and ready when a death-facing defense of his lord was required. It was warrior against warrior, cutting viciously with the sword, with little regard for broader definitions of justice or of mercy. The movies do not paint an altogether false picture and, even if we add a sensitivity to the arts and a steadfast scrupulousness in the way in which battle is engaged, the result is nothing like the "spiritual path" which *aikidō* describes. But if we compare the European knight of faith and the Japanese samurai warrior, as Saotome suggests, we find that "for both . . . a code of ethics was held as the ideal. This chivalrous way was based on loyalty and honor, selflessness and duty, and an attitude which came very close to a worship of the sword, the glistening steel of death. Yet in Japan ideals like these were refined to a depth that affects the consciousness of the nation still" (Saotome 1993, 104). Training in this unflinching way of facing life's challenges is still very often a part of corporate education for success in business and industry. One well-known leader of industry, both in Japan and in the West, told me of his first day on the job with a major Japanese corporation—one which he was still employed by as he approached his retirement—when the company's president called him into his office and told him that his first job was to read through the file of a company with which they had done business for nearly two decades and answer the query which they had sent. Delighted by the attention of the president, he spent the morning thoroughly digesting the file and, as the day closed, he had a draft among many drafts of a letter which he thought was ready. The president read the response letter, handed it back, and said, "No! This will not do." There were no further instructions. He took the file home, wrote draft letters through the night, and by morning had a second draft ready for the president. "No!" said the president, dismissing him with a wave of his hand. This incredible trial by fire continued for eighteen days, as I recall the story, and throughout that time there were no further instructions. It was up to this new recruit to find out for himself what was needed, for there was no formula, only a product that would suit this particular occasion. On the eighteenth day, by now wondering how soon he would be walking the sidewalks again in search of a new job, he took a draft to the president, who this time said, "Yes! Yes! Now write all your letters like this!" Evidently he did so, for when I met him, he had been the senior president of several major subsidiary companies of this larger company. It is samurai-like toughening that was employed, together with a lesson in intuiting the correct approach, an approach which is not situation specific, but which is deep enough in one's understanding to be applicable to any and all situations which might arise. My friend was on a quest for excellence in business, the European knight was fighting for the Christian God and, hence, was on a spiritual quest which he understood to be of considerable merit, and the Japanese samurai was embodying steadfast loyalty and respect for his superior. To be anything less, one would not be a Japanese samurai. However, beginning in the thirteenth century, the samurai tradition became increasingly influenced by the teachings of Zen Buddhism, and a gentler view of *budō* began to emerge. The great emphasis on training, in both traditions, led to a remarkably easy evolutionary transition. D. T. Suzuki wrote that:

> *Bushido*, as we generally understand it now, is the act of being an unflinching guardian-god of the dignity of the samurai, and this dignity consists in loyalty, filial piety, and benevolence. But to fulfill these duties successfully two things are needed: to train oneself in moral asceticism, not only in its practical aspect but in its philosophical preparation; and to be always ready to face death, that is, to sacrifice oneself unhesitatingly when occasion arises. To do this, much mental and spiritual training is needed. (Suzuki 1959, 70)

Suzuki adds that there are specific aspects of Zen which were especially congenial to the development of a samurai: (1) "Zen upholds intuition against intellection"; (2) "Zen discipline is simple, direct, self-reliant, self-denying"; and (3) it emphasizes the singular importance of will power (Suzuki 1959, 61–62).

Yagyu

It might well be claimed that the spirit of *budō* as a truly self-cultivational path was forged at Yagyu, a small, sleepy village just south of Kyoto. Hotokuzen-ji, which dates from 1638, is a Zen Buddhist temple that was also a center for training in the sword, and to this day is still a center for the study and practice of *kendō*.[7] The Yagyu area was heavily involved in fighting during the civil war from 1467–1477 (Wars of Ōnin). Out of this memory arose the Shinkage school or tradition of swordsmanship that began to seek ways of peacemaking, rather than warmaking. Hotokuzen-ji was not only the center of the new *budō*, but it was also the family Temple of the Yagyū clan, and founded by the Zen priest Takuan, whose famous letter to Yagyū Munenori,[8] Lord of Tajima, still stands as prime evidence of the profound link between Zen philosophy and the changing art of swordsmanship. D. T. Suzuki states that Takuan's letter includes the essential teachings of Zen, as well as the "secrets" of the artistic "ways":

> In Japan, perhaps as in other countries too, mere technical knowledge of an art is not enough to make a man really its master; he ought to have delved deeply into the inner spirit of it. This spirit is grasped only when his mind is in complete harmony with the principle of life itself, that is, when he attains to a certain state of mind known as *mushin* . . . "no-mind." In Buddhist phraseology, it means going beyond the dualism of all forms of life and death, good and evil, being and non-being. This is where all arts merge into Zen. (Suzuki 1959, 94)

The central message is that, in whatever you are engaged, it is imperative to forget your conscious mind and to become one with the challenge at hand. In doing so, the action will spring

---

7. The term *kendō* refers to the relatively modern, sportive version using split bamboo swords. The main, older, generic Japanese designation of swordsmanship was *kenjutsu*, "sword art," which was a warrior fighting skill.

8. Tajima no kami was Iemitsu's (the third *shōgun* of the Tokugawa era) teacher of swordsmanship, and studied Zen under Takuan (the abbot of Daitoku-ji, in Kyoto).

directly from one's unconscious, seemingly effortlessly and certainly intuitively, and far more quickly than the conscious, deliberative mind could act. As *budō* became increasingly influenced by Zen, the conclusion was eventually reached, at least by some, that human beings should no longer try to solve their problems by the sword, for Zen taught a far different state of awareness. This new mentality was a gentler form of *budō*.

In my visit to the ancient temple at Yagyu, the head priest, Hashimoto-sensei, stressed that the change from the actual sword to the split-bamboo "sword" (*shinai*) best represents this change in mentality. He handed me the *shinai*, which was swordlike in length, but the end was split or cut into several strands up what would have been the blade, yielding a broken sound when struck. This practice sword does everything but cut and is still the sword used in training and competition in *kendō*. He added that "the idea now is that swords should be carried, but not used. Ultimately, it was thought, one could defend oneself without using the sword." The aim of training became one of not-hurting, of self-protection rather than aggression. *Kendō* became a defensive, rather than an offensive, art. Insightfully, he pointed out that what *kendō* teaches is a living *kōan*, i.e., a paradox or puzzle that cannot be solved rationally: "through the sword, how is non-aggressive peace to be established?" The answer must be that one uses the sword not as a sword. Just as Zen uses the mind to create no-mind through meditation, so no-mind in *budō* manifests as the sword which is no-sword. And the upshot of such practice is that "one learns how one should live with others. The other becomes a partner, rather than an opponent." "*Shugyō*," he added, "becomes interrelational *shugyō*, or ethics, and not just personal practice. This sense of *shugyō* includes learning to live non-aggressively with others, being able to see the 'other' as a partner rather than an opponent; the 'other' comes to be seen as bestowed with infinite worth." But first, "one must purify oneself, cleanse oneself, get rid of the clutter, and then the world of everyday experience is fresh each and every moment."

During my visit at Yagyu, I had the privilege of interviewing two women, each of whom was a distinguished and widely recognized master of a martial art. Hasegawa Hideko, now very elderly, is a master of *bōjutsu* (the art of the six-foot-long staff) and the first woman to reach the level of master. Ichiba Tomiko is a master of *naginata* (the sword on a pole) and the second woman to reach the master level. Both demonstrated their arts out of doors and were truly astounding. I kept dodging the day's drying laundry on the line, as I backed up to take another unforgettable picture of these two magnificent and tender women at work. Later, seated in the raised living room of the old farmhouse in the center of the tiny village, surrounded by hills and working rice paddies, the conversation led to a heartfelt discussion of the martial arts, and of the current state of Japanese society. Both masters were in full agreement in insisting that practice must begin and end with meditation; that the skills learned are to be used for self-protection only; that *satori* is to be found in following a martial path; and that along the way, one learns good attitudes, a powerful sense of compassion, and the preciousness of each and every moment. Practice in technique produces an expanded *kokoro* (mind/heart), yielding both kindness and calmness, an increase in sensitivity toward others, respect, viewing the "other" as a partner assisting in one's development, and a very strong desire to help others grow and spiritually mature.

Both masters emphasized that today there is a profound confusion between practice and training. Training (*keiko*) is more like sport, whereas true practice (*shugyō*), involves the whole person; body, mind, and spirit. "The mind is in the body—practice is necessary to refine both the mind and the body," continued Iehiba-sensei. And the ultimate result hoped for is *satori*, which is a change in one's *kokoro*. She recounted that as she advanced in the *naginata*, she was able to experience things which she could never have imagined before. "Everything was new, as though somehow transformed before my eyes," and she had an intensely strong desire to share this "feeling," this change in perception and way-of-being with others.

This distinction between training (*keiko*) and twenty-four-hour-a-day practice in personality development (*shugyō*) with total commitment is crucial in distinguishing the *dō*, martial and nonmartial, from sports. *Keiko* refers to "the present training session," or to working on specific skills or muscle groups. *Shugyō* is a lifelong endeavor or activity. Furthermore, *aikidō*, for the most part, does not employ competition although, as is well known, much that passes for the martial arts is heavily involved in competition. By contrast, "*aikidō* was developed for

communication, not competition" (Saotome 1993, 136). Saotome, in contrasting the martial arts with sport writes that:

> Teaching a competitive martial way is not the teach-
> ing of truth. Competition can be a constructive and pos-
> itive outlet for our aggressions. It can shake us from our
> complacency and push us to do things we never would
> have tried, make us go a little farther or run just a little
> faster. This is the desired result of games and sport. But
> Budō is not a game. Budō is a way of life, a life attitude.
> The reason behind the supreme effort must be different.
> When competition becomes excessive and becomes the
> driving force in daily life as it has in much of modern so-
> ciety, it breeds more frustration, distorting the person-
> ality and destroying human relationships. . . . The ego
> rears its ugly head and says, "I'm better than you. I want
> you to know it, and I'm going to prove it." And compe-
> tition, no longer an outlet for aggression, becomes an act
> of aggression. (Saotome 1993, 136)

Saotome concludes that most of the modern styles of the martial
arts have veered so far from the *budō* ideal that they have "lost
their essence." In fact, the application of the arts has narrowed,
"now concerned with victory and defeat." *Aikidō*, as *budō*, is
not sport, but a sustained and mindful way to develop oneself as
a whole human being.[9] The goal of practice in *budō* is to control
and eliminate aggressive responses, whereas:

> sports-oriented martial arts concentrate on aggression,
> on the negative aspects of defeating the enemy. You can-
> not control the reactions of another through aggression,
> for aggression only draws more resistance. If you push,
> you create a situation in which the other can resist your
> power, and it becomes a struggle decided by physical
> strength. But if the other pushes, and you are flexible

---

9. Most modern *budō* (*judō, karatedō, kendō, kyodō, naginata*, etc.) do have a
strong sportive or competitive component, but most still strive to go far beyond
that to the highest ideals of *budō*.

enough to turn without hesitation rather than resist, the
other will be drawn into the vacuum you have created
and be within your sphere of control. This cannot be
accomplished only with the physical body; it must be
directed by spiritual attitude.

The goal of Budo training, of Aikidō training, is not
to magnify aggressive response but to control and refine
it. We must learn to appreciate the process that leads to
the true wisdom of harmony. Sports championship is
only small entertainment. The Way of Bu teaches us to
throw away private ambition and greed and to become
empty. (Saotome 1993, 138)

Therefore, it must be stressed that *budō*, and specifically *aikidō*,
are educational formats for training the mind, body, and spirit.
"Physical technique is not the true object, but a tool for personal
refinement and spiritual growth" (Saotome 1993, 245). In sum,
the *dōjō* is not a gymnasium, but "a place for uplifting and
cleansing one's body, mind, and spirit," a place where it is para-
mount that one display "the correct attitude of respect, sincerity,
and modesty," qualities that are not always evident in the sports
arenas of today (Saotome 1993, 245).

Letting Go of the Ego

As we began our week of practice at the Ki Society headquarters,
the calligraphy on the front wall read, "Blessed universal spirit,
we feel your presence." This sentiment is affirmed by Tohei
through what he terms the principle of non-dissension, which
teaches the importance of avoiding aggression in any of its
forms. Dissension arises when we dualistically split off from the
oneness of the universal, and we lapse "into the attitude that
fighting is the natural thing, that this is indeed a world of jungle
law" (Tohei 1966, 155). There is almost always a way to avoid
fighting. Idealistically, Tohei concludes that "if fighting is not in
our hearts we have neither foes nor allies because all of us are
brothers born of the *ki* of the universe" (Tohei 1966, 162–63).
Again, contrasting *aikidō* with sports, he writes that sports usually "enjoy encouragement, technical progress, and popularity
from matches of one sort or another," but *aikidō* "matches are

not permitted . . . because, unlike sports, *aikidō* walks the way of the universal and has as its sole aim the perfection of mankind" (Tohei 1966, 163).[10] Furthermore:

> In the first place, *aikidō* is a discipline designed to penetrate to the inner meaning of the principle of non-dissension. In matches, someone must win, and winning in itself implies a heart filled with fighting. If you strive with all your might to win, it is doubtless very fine for your sportsmanship, but with the burning desire to be victorious you may develop the psychology that any means is all right if it helps you win. This attitude can do great harm to you as a person. (Tohei 1966, 163)

Tohei goes so far as to claim that if you are unable to understand and master the principle of non-dissension, "you will be unable to master the techniques." The ultimate victory sought is a victory over oneself (*agatsu*), and there are more than enough matches to be involved in within yourself to keep you going for a lifetime. Maintain the one point, extend *ki*, and thereby maintain your constant equilibrium. This is where the testing, which Tohei has added to *aikidō*'s repertoire, comes to the fore. By lightly touching a person on any one of a number of locations on the body—the shoulder, the upper chest, the arm, the knee, the elbow, etc.—one can determine whether or not the one point is being maintained. It is a measure of one's *ki*, and it is almost like magic, but it works. To my mind this is his greatest contribution to *aikidō*, and it is of immense importance. The purpose of testing—a gentle push to

---

10. "*Aikidō* prohibits matches because permitting them would result in a departure from the true meaning of *budō*. On the other hand, almost everyone has some sort of desire to improve, as well as to compete; these are what stimulate us to make efforts and give us hope that we can develop ourselves. *Aikidō* prohibits matches because matches are concerned with the issue of winning or losing. There would be no problem if matches were not about victory and defeat, but rather about how much we can unify the mind we have been given by heaven and earth to discover our fullest potential as human beings. With this in mind I established what we call the *Shin Shin Toitsu Aikidō* Competition, an event not for displays of circus-like techniques or other curiosities, but rather an opportunity to test this mind-body unification that anyone has the potential to attain. This event is not limited to *Ki* Society members, anyone can participate. But those unable to unify their mind and body won't get very far in the competition" (Tohei 1996b, 4).

determine whether one is solidly positioned—is to help one learn to extend one's *ki*, to improve mind/body coordination, and to learn to relax. *Ki*-testing is an external mirror, a confirmation of what is actually happening. Its purpose is to help the person being tested to improve. There is no pass or fail grade: it is a check-up, a barometer of one's *ki* flow. It is not merely a measure of where you are, but an incentive to advance, to improve. Since you cannot detect or sense the mind with the five senses, the state of one's mind can only be determined by checking the state of one's body. It is emphasized over and over again that you cannot test another if you have a "selfish mind," i.e., if you are self-focused, rather than other focused. While at World Camp, we were taught the "ethics" of testing: it must always be a mutual undertaking and never just one-sided; a person is expected to envelop another with one's "plus mind" in the testing (rather than fearing that the other will prove to be better, or hoping that she or he will fail for whatever reason); and there must be a scrupulous desire to be fair and to respect a partner's bodymind. The person testing should not hesitate in touching and pushing, for when you hesitate, your mind stops. Nor should the person being tested focus on the point of contact, for that, too, stops *ki*, or places it at the point of touch, rather than on relaxing, extending *ki*, and remaining one-pointed. The sword always cuts, and so, even in testing we should always display mind-body coordination. Remarkably, our minds will change unconsciously through *ki* testing. It is a vital part of *aikidō* practice and not an examination of some kind which is separate from it. It is a vital part of the learning and a vital ingredient in self-cultivation. Thinking negatively actually stops the flow of *ki*; thinking positively increases its flow, for to think positively is actually to extend one's *ki*. Negative thoughts and even negative words, set up blocking patterns in one's unconscious mind.

The principle of non-dissension is a crucial ethical teaching. Like Gandhi's non-violence and Albert Schweitzer's reverence for life, it stands as a searchlight by means of which one can determine the extent of one's resolve, understanding, and courage. It is a rule of sorts, but like so many ethical teachings in Japan, it is more a matter of attitudes than it is about moral law or ethical normative specificity. If one knows one's kinship with all that exists, then one's attitudinal stance *must* be one of love, compassion, and the protection of all that exists, to the extent that this is possible. Once we recognize that we are one with the universe, the reflection of the universe that appears in the divine soul is always in the form of love. It is a manifestation of the spirit that says we must love, protect, and nurture all things. It is, therefore, incumbent upon us not to fight (unless there is no other alternative, and even then it is "fighting" with the purpose of helping the other person, i.e., not allowing the other to hurt or be hurt), not to focus on winning or losing, not to egoistically rank oneself as superior, or as a superstar, but rather to "correct each other as whetstones, and mirror each other's actions" (Tohei 1966, 106–07). Furthermore, "*aikidō* is the spirit of love and protection for all things; it is the spirit of peace" (Tohei 1966, 197).

Other character traits, or attitudes, are also mentioned along the way: openness, frankness, humility, perseverance, generosity, courtesy, harmony, fearlessness, wisdom, friendship, reconciliation, cooperation, empathy, respect, patience, having a calm mind, and being in control of one's anger. This focus is on character development, personal growth, and spiritual realization, i.e., a reminder that I am already divine, and so are you, and that we are, always have been, and always will be one with the universal which sustains us. *Aikidō* practice, technique, breathing, and testing are all aimed at bringing this realization to a constant state of awareness, and this understanding is the basis on which one now seeks to act.

The *aikidō* way of ethical living, then, is rather simple, although achieving it requires sincere effort over a lifetime, it is never fully completed and, hence, is ever in progress: "Those who are enlightened never stop forging themselves" (Ueshiba 1992, 52). But it all begins with the one point as the reservoir of *ki* energy. While there is much speculation about what *ki* is, and even whether such an energy even exists, the focus on one point brings incredible results in the form of magnified power. Continual training and testing is necessary in order to both intensify the flow of *ki* and render it increasingly constant.

As you become aware of your connection to the universal, a sense of compassion and love emerges, not only with respect to others—now viewed as partners, rather than as strangers or opponents—but also with respect to nature in all its forms. One's stance in the world is now positive, "plus rather than minus," and one is empowered to make a difference in the world, to affect others positively. And even though one may be approaching the status of an *aikidō* master, capable of what seems to outsiders to be "superhuman" power, one is a peacemaker, dedicated to stopping aggression rather than adding to it. For me, one of the most vivid memories of my stay at World Camp was a demonstration of disarming one who had attacked with a sword (or knife, or gun). It was done so quickly and smoothly that it was almost quicker than the eye. But the greatest surprise was yet to come: the weapon was not then directed at the attacker, now flat on his back, but rather was kept hidden behind the *aikidōka*. To use it as it was used is to further the aggression. To hide it is to defuse the power of the weapon and, hopefully, to defuse aggression altogether. The aim is to de-escalate the situation and make room for peace. John Stevens, quoting Ueshiba-sensei, sums up this dedication to peace and to making a difference in the world:

> Unlike the authors of old-time warrior classics such as *The Art of War* and *The Book of Five Rings*, which accept the inevitability of war and emphasize cunning strategy as a means to victory, Morihei understood that continued fighting—with others, with ourselves, and with the environment—will ruin the earth. "The world will continue to change dramatically, but fighting and war can destroy us utterly. What we need now are techniques of harmony, not those of contention. The Art of Peace is required, not the Art of War." . . . Everyone can be a warrior for peace. (Ueshiba 1992, 8–9)

Each of us can and should "be transformed into goddesses of compassion or victorious buddhas," for the divine is not something high above us. It is in heaven, it is in earth, it is inside us" (Ueshiba 1992, 117–19). *Aikidō* offers the power of transformation on an individual basis, but it can also positively affect families, communities, and even beyond.

CHAPTER THREE

Landscape Gardening as Interconnectedness

Prelude

In his essay on the German poet Goethe, the Japanese philosopher Nishida Kitarō emphasizes that Western art has *form* as its focus, whereas Eastern art expresses both *form* and the *formless*. He refers to the formless aspect as the "background" of things, and this background "is an integral part" of art worthy of the name. Using a sculptor's image, he imagines "all great art" as a relief "cut out of the marble of eternity," as Michelangelo released David from the stone in which he was held fast (Nishida 1976, 145). In more formal philosophical language, the background is "absolute nothingness," that formless, quality-less "no-thing" out of which all forms arise and to which they will all return. Nothingness is the creative matrix which exists prior to form, and like the eye which can see all things seeable but which cannot see itself, so nothingness is the origin of all form (things), but itself is formless. The formless cannot be seen (directly), and yet, for the discerning mind and heart, it can be seen (indirectly) in every thing. Nothingness is eternity at "the back of things" (Nishida 1976, 146). Furthermore, each and every moment is "a determination" of "the eternal Now," a coming-to-be-formed that arose out of the formless eternity of absolute existence (Nishida 1976, 158). Nishida's description of a common understanding in the Far East, is that of ultimate reality as a pulsating energy field which self-expresses by congealing in places, producing formed things. Creation is not to be thought of as something apart from this creative force, nor is that which is created to be thought of as separate

51

from this creative force. Nothingness, like a pulsating energy field gives birth to things, the formless self-manifests as form, and eternity now expresses itself in time. Everything that is, is a manifestation of the divine: every thing is divine, although more often than not, totally unaware of its divine origin, and of the divine origin of all other things. Nothingness is, then, a great formless reservoir of potential and actual forms.

The artist both intuits this connection between time and eternity and expresses it in and through his or her artistic medium. Art is not merely the object or performance but must also include a glimpse of the whole of which it is an expression in this moment, in the now.

The inclusion of the formless, of eternity, of nothingness is what gives great art depth, and as Nishida's essay indicates, this deep profundity is not limited to the East. He cites Rembrandt, some Christian artists and writers and, of course, Goethe as artists who represented something more than pure form. But it is in Eastern art, and in Japanese art in particular, that this unity of time and eternity, the formed and the formless, has come to be regarded as essential. The Zen scholar Hisamatsu Shin'ichi has described this requirement of the inclusion of "background" or "depth" in Japanese art as "subtle profundity or deep reserve" (Hisamatsu 1982, 33). Just as a person who shows true humility appears to be quite ordinary in the way she or he lives and interacts with others, while simultaneously being recognized by many in the outside world as an extraordinary person, so great art does not thrust itself forward in an attempt to reveal all, but instead "all is not disclosed, something infinite is contained" (Hisamatsu 1982, 33). The result of this reserve is an inexhaustability, the kind that brings you back again and again to a great piece of literature, or music, or painting, or pottery bowl, and each time one is greeted with a freshness which reveals what had not been seen before. One experiences "an endless reverberation, which comes from a never completely revealed, bottomless depth" (Hisamatsu 1982, 34). This is not coyness, but the result of our inability to actually express the inexpressible, or to give form to the formless. All that can be done is to point, to gesture toward the infinite depth in the background of the foreground object of art in question: it is a calling to attention, a turning of the mind and heart toward the unseen and eternal inexhaustability of ultimate reality.

This object or performance is an "image of eternity," and it is "mirrored in eternity" (Nishida 1976, 145). Because the eternal is included in truly profound artistic expression, even if only as a subtle gesture pointing to the "background," it produces in our hearts "a formless, boundless vibration, and an endless, voiceless echo" (Nishida 1976, 146). In other words, we resonate to and with the art object or performance, and somehow we hear the voice of eternity without actually, physically hearing it. Art lifts each person who responds, who "hears," to a new level of awareness and possibility, to a new or renewed level of living and acting, for one now intuits the connection between time and eternity, the formed and the formless, the part and the whole. In this very important sense, art can be transformative. It elicits the depth in the heart and mind of the observer, taking one a step closer to enlightened awareness. Art moves one beyond surface living, to living in three dimensions. Its purpose is to render one whole, able to see things holistically.

In addition to "subtle profundity or deep reserve," Hisamatsu lists six other characteristics of Japanese aesthetic sensibility: (1) asymmetry, (2) simplicity, (3) austere sublimity or lofty dryness, (4) naturalness, (5) freedom from attachment, and (6) tranquility. In the great gardens of Japan, all seven qualities are in evidence (Hisamatsu 1982).

Anyone who stands before a painting by Rembrandt or Van Gogh, or is enveloped at a concert by the music of Bach or Beethoven, or who enters a Japanese landscape garden risks such transformation. It is not just a matter of paint, or musical instruments, or stones and plants, but of giving voice to a higher and deeper awareness through the forms that are at our disposal. The artist gives voice to the voiceless in art, and the artist's voice is a voice of the absolute, of Buddha, of the divine, of God. In this very real sense, God or the absolute is directly underfoot and all around us. From the Zen Buddhist perspective, the absolute is within, and one's task as an artist and as a human being is to somehow get what is inside, outside. A work of art is the merging of subject and object in an attempt to express the beautiful and the sublime: the formed (the beautiful) and the formless (the sublime).

As one enters a landscape garden there is a break with the everyday "flatland" of ordinary life and an entry into a multidimensional landscape of profound meaning and depth. It is as though one were given new eyes with which to see the world. The greens are more vivid, and yet, at the same time, more subdued, more subtle. The silence only serves to heighten each and every sound: the cicadas buzzing their song, a tiny stream gurgling in the distance, the whispers of other visitors. In a green, moss-covered garden where the moss forms the "background" for the foreground plants, trees, and rocks, one can smell the damp mustiness of the varieties of moss and the soil beneath, or a new fungus, freshly pungent from the rain the night before which gave it birth. The dappled patterns of sunlight breaking through the canopy of trees create a dark-brightness, a subdued atmosphere punctuated with bursts of bright sunlight on a patch of moss, a flowering shrub, or a single rock at the edge of a pond. Suddenly the world is an enchanted world, and as with all enchantment, one is taken out of oneself, one forgets oneself to be placed in a richer and more congenial and more profound world. One is not only in the garden, but now one is a part of the garden: not a visitor any longer, but a participant. The garden, too, is more than a garden, for it is an expression of eternity, of the absolute. Individuality has been added and is joined by profound connections with the entire world of nature and with the universe as a whole, both the seen and the unseen. In the most profound sense, one will never be the same again.

The Shintō Influence

Landscape gardens are of many kinds and attract thousands of Japanese each year. There are several styles of gardens in Japan and striking differences even within these "kinds." Stroll gardens feature large ponds with islands. Pure Land Buddhist stroll gardens emphasize the journey from one side of the pond to the other, where the temple is located that represents Heaven or the Pure Land. Meditation gardens are small Zen gardens, featuring white sand or gravel as the base cover representing nothingness, the formless, and the "background," raked in various patterns, and usually, although not always, numerous larger stones are nestled in the sand. These two are of two kinds: internal (as in Zen temples or tea rooms), and external, adjacent to the main building, with a platform for meditation. Some meditation gardens include plant material, and the whole effect represents in three dimensions the classic Chinese landscape painting (in two dimensions). Tea gardens, surrounding a tea house or hut, are meant to prepare the participant-guests spiritually as they move at a leisurely pace toward the tea event. The more austere and remarkably abstract Zen rock gardens have come to symbolize the uniqueness of the Japanese perspective on gardens. Whether one takes the most abstract rock garden of them all, at Ryoan-ji, in Kyoto, which consists of fifteen large rocks emerging out of a "sea" or "background" of (formless) sand, or more complex "dry rock paintings" which mimic Chinese landscape paintings (Daisen-in, interior garden), or a meditation garden which consists only of a field of sand raked into two small Fuji-shaped cones (Daisen-in, exterior garden), there is nothing quite like these expressions of the formless and the formed in other cultural traditions. If you will imagine the two cone-shaped forms emerging out of the sand background, each composed of the very sand which represents formlessness, then you may also understand how "empty" (in the sense of temporary and fragile) forms really are. A quick swipe of a rake or an arm, and the cones are gone, returned to the background from which they came. Moreover, the monk-gardener can quickly re-create the two cones, or many more if he chooses, by giving shape to the background sand once more. What becomes evident in this example in that the foreground cones are of the same stuff as the background whole— form is emptiness, emptiness form; or, in more traditional Buddhist terms, *nirvāna* is *samsāra*, *samsāra* is *nirvāna*.

The Japanese love of nature serves as the bridge which takes us from nature itself to gardens as ideal representations. The prominence of rocks, too, has a long ancestry. Berthier remarks that the delight which the Japanese take in rocks spawned the belief that high mountains, where rocks abound in their untouched state, "were places impregnated by supernatural forces," or in Shintō places where the *kami* are likely to be found. *Kami*, or the "gods" (not an acceptable translation of *kami*, which refers to the awesome, the mysterious, the powerful, or any place where an outbreak of intense and concentrated energy may be felt) are to be found in greater concentration in the hills and mountains, still considered to be sacred places. The *kami* tend to manifest in natural places or things, which in turn are thought of as sacred objects (Berthier 2000, 43). Japan boasts literally tens of thousands of *torii*, the bright orange-red gateways which announce the presence of the awesome, the magnificent, the mysterious, whether it be a sunset, a waterfall, an old tree, a rock or gathering of rocks, or a rushing river. The *torii* are eye-catching exclamation points, calling attention to the presence of the divine. In addition to the *torii* gateway, there is also the *shimenawa*, a twisted rope made of new rice straw tied around a rock or a tree, indicating a sacred space or object. Pockets of great energy, or awesome beauty, or remarkableness are to be found virtually anywhere in nature. The world of nature in particular is simply alive with the awesome, the magnificent, the powerful (a thundering waterfall, for example), and the breathtakingly beautiful.

The Shintō view of creation does not begin with a creator who decided to make a universe, but rather, the heretofore totally unseen and unformed (without form) simply manifests as form. There was first pure subjectivity; the unseen and not yet objectified (no-thing). Subjectivity then objectified, that is to say the non-material materialized or congealed, and the unseen became seeable, the formless took form. Since all form is a self-expression of the initially sacred subjectivity as formless, then everything that exists is divine. Everything that has taken form, including human beings, "share one and the same divine blood which flows through animals, plants, minerals and all other things in Nature" (Herbert 1967, 21). Shintō has found divinity in every possible natural entity at some point in its history: from "wind, thunder, lightening, rain, the sun, mountains, rivers, trees, and rocks" to remarkable human beings and their work (Parkes 1997, 113). One who works in and with nature is working with *kami*, the divine, and as such is engaged in a spiritual practice. This is exactly the atmosphere in which the landscape gardener is immersed: and a similar story must be told from the Buddhist perspective, as will be seen shortly. Shintō's reverence and respect for nature as a self-manifestation of the divine energy of continual creation certainly serves as hospitable soil for the influx of landscape gardens from China. Shintō shrines themselves are usually surrounded by a rectangular area of sand or fine stone, usually white, with only a cherry, plum, or a pine tree or two to break the expanse which symbolizes nothingness and purity. It is but a small step from the rectangular sand spaces of Shintō to the stone gardens of Zen.

The Buddhist Influence

While a good deal of the background to landscape gardening in Japan is Shintō, certainly it is Buddhism that provides the shape and form of the various types of landscape design. Buddhism and Zen Buddhism are major contributors to the Japanese understanding of the importance of, and the designing of landscape gardens. Most of the finest existing examples of landscape gardens are to be found in Buddhist and Zen Buddhist temples and their grounds. Thomas Hoover observes that "for at least a millennium before the coming of Zen to Japan, gardens had been constructed in China which were founded on underlying religious motives, but only with the rise of Zen in medieval Japan did gardens become deliberately symbolic of the human quest for inner understanding" (Hoover 1977, 85). The keystones to this transformation were the emphasis on meditation, and the belief in the sanctity of all that exists. As early as the eighth century, *Tiantai* (*Tendai* in Japan) Buddhism in China expanded the Buddhist belief that all sentient beings have Buddha-nature to include non-sentient beings as well, such as plants, trees, the soil, and even "a tiny particle of dust" (Zhanran, *Jigang Bi*, as cited in Fung 1953, 385–86). This way of thinking about the universal existence of Buddha-nature had a significant impact upon the way in which gardens and their materials were understood. Parkes chronicles the history of this belief from Saichō (766–822—founder of the Tendai school of Buddhism in Japan), who was the first in Japan to affirm the "Buddha-nature of trees and rocks," to Kukai (774–835), who proclaimed that sentient and non-sentient beings alike were the body of the Buddha, of the Divine, to the great Zen master Dōgen, who translated the statement made in the *Nirvāna Sūtra* that "all sentient beings without exception have Buddha-nature" as "all is sentient being, all beings are Buddha-nature" (Parkes 1997, 113–16). It is in and through the natural landscape that the self-realized soul can read, as Dōgen writes, "Buddha's shape, form, and voice" (cited in Parkes 1997, 117). Nature can be read as scripture if one has the heart and mind to see what is there before one. We need to be open to the natural environment and learn to listen to its teachings as a "non-sentient's dharma-discourse," that is, as the true teachings of Buddha himself (Kim 1985, 262). Indeed, Dōgen takes us yet one step further, by actually going beyond "the distinction between sentient and non-sentient beings," for he claims that even "walls and tiles, mountains, rivers, and the great earth" are also to be included (Parkes 1997, 123). Thus, not only natural, but even human-made objects are to be considered as participating in the divinity of existence, and presumably are to be treated with respect precisely because they are sacred objects.

Dōgen's remarkable essay "Valley Sounds, Mountain Sights" (*Keiseisanshoku*) emphasizes that the animate and inanimate in nature all speak, and they all speak, in their depths, the truth of existence. He laments that "we so often seem left out of the transformative process of the dharma-discourse through the Buddha's manifested body," and in so doing he makes clear that the world as the manifestation of the ultimate energy is capable of transforming us, if we but listen to its murmurings (Kim 1985, 261). In this sense, "mountains and waters of themselves become wise ones and sages": they become our teachers (Kim 1985, 302).

Landscape gardens in Japan are inspired by Shintō, Tiantai and Pure Land Buddhism, and Zen Buddhism. However, the development of Japan's rock gardens are almost completely the product of Zen Buddhism, albeit resting on the long history of garden-making both in China and in Japan. Yet even here the tendrils of influence are greater than might be noticed at first. It will be recalled that Shintō, from its beginning, thought of rocks as particularly auspicious habitats for *kami*, and "it was a natural step to then supplement nature by building piles of rocks to attract *kami* to a particular place, and these became the prototypes of the arrangements that would grace Japanese gardens in later centuries" (Parkes 2002, 46). In Japan's first, and most well known, manual of landscape gardening, *Sakuteiki*, written nearly a thousand years ago, the author instructs that one must take care in choosing and setting stones in place in landscape and dry landscape gardens: "Choose a particularly splendid stone and set it as the Main Stone. Then, following the request of the first stone, set others accordingly" (Takei and Keene 2001, 183). It would be all too easy to skip over this instruction as a rather quaint way of telling the reader to pay particular attention to the choosing and laying of the first or main stone. Yet, as will be demonstrated by the contemporary Zen landscape designer, Masuno Shunmyo, who was mentioned in chapter 1, it is absolutely imperative that one take this instruction to heart in an utterly literal way: pay attention to the "request" of the first stone, and, of course, to all other stones, plants, fences, tiles, waterfalls, and the site on which all of these are to be placed. A dialogue must be established with each and every one of these ingredients if the result is to be both natural, and spiritually instructive. In Western cultural climates, one would be looked at with the greatest of suspicion upon speaking of initiating a dialogue with rocks and plants. You would be smiled upon as "weird" or "flaky," or frowned upon as at least slightly pathological. Yet Masuno insists that without such a dialogue, true Zen garden-making is simply impossible, and the results would inevitably be less than satisfying aesthetically and spiritually.

Zen-Inspired Gardens

The dry landscape garden (*kare sansui*), fashioned only of sand, stone, and possibly, but not necessarily, a sparse inclusion of plant life, is considered by many to be the pinnacle of landscape gardening. The most abstract garden of them all, at Ryoan-ji, consists of a vast expanse of sand, on which are set (yet which seem to grow out of and to recede into the sand "canvas") fifteen rocks arranged in a compelling manner conveying great age. Some of the rocks are embedded in moss, which extends slightly beyond the rock-footprints. One could settle onto the viewing platform along one side of the garden and try to take all of it in over several hours of meditation and aesthetic delight. Each stone seems to have been placed exactly where it ought to have been placed, is of the right size and shape, and is set at just the right level with respect to the sand bed on which it rests. Once, after having just come from several hours at the garden's side, I was welcomed into the home of the distinguished Zen Buddhist philosopher, Nishitani Keiji, in Kyoto. He asked where I was coming from, and when I told him about my visit to Ryoan-ji, he quickly asked whether I had heard the garden roar. Zen gardens are, supposedly, so authentic in their dry waterfalls and dry riverbeds that a keen listener can hear the roar of the water. On a later visit to his home, he returned to Ryoan-ji as a topic, and this time further elaborated that most people who visit the great landscape gardens merely "look at the surface . . . at the beautiful rocks, the rippled patterns in the sand, the moss, and the earth-colored walls. But the garden is the expression of the landscape architect's own enlightenment! . . . Underneath our feet [if we imagine ourselves back at Ryoan-ji], where we are, at this place, the garden is looking at us, for we are now a part of the actual manifestation of the garden architect's own enlightenment experience. The garden is my Zen master now, and it is your Zen master, too." The garden can be a source of our own personal self-transformation, if we will let it, for it is an expression of the self-transformation of the master architect. It is so much more than a simple selection of interesting stones, cleverly arranged, like a paper collage.

Perhaps the foregoing will serve as the background for my encounter with the landscape architect, Masuno Shunmyo, at his temple in Yokohama. I first learned of Masuno from a close friend in construction, and philosophy, who had befriended colleagues who were involved in the building of the *Zen Garden* at the Canadian Museum of Civilization in Ottawa, Canada. The museum officials had chosen Masuno Shunmyo to build a Zen-style garden, which was to be located on a public terrace rooftop, adjacent to the main entrance. He was greeted at the airport by those assigned to meet him and escort him and his crew to the future garden site for a brief "get-acquainted" visit, and then take him to his hotel. He was dressed in his Sōtō Zen robes, his head shaved bald, and wearing glasses. It was late afternoon, a typically frigid day in late autumn with the temperature below freezing. He arrived at the site, studied it closely, and sat down immediately to survey the future garden area. The daylight was fast disappearing, and his reception committee asked if it was time to make their way to his hotel room. Focused on the site, and already making mental notes and plans, he informed them that he would not be needing a hotel room for he would spend the night at the site. They insisted that it was to be an uncomfortably cold night, that snow was predicted, but he assured them that he would be fine, and that it was imperative that he begin his work at once.

The reception committee returned early the next morning, fearing that an international incident might well be brewing because of the untimely death of a landscape architect from Japan, who was left to freeze at the Museum of Civilization. What they actually found was a priest-designer, not only comfortable, but eager to show them the sketch he had completed of the garden plans. Astonished as they were, there was still more to come. Not only had he sketched out the initial design, but he had sketched as well the shape, size, and estimated weight of each of the rocks which would be required. Together with his associates from Japan and the museum officials, he set out to locate the right rocks for the garden. He recalls that this was no easy task, but eventually the proper rocks for the project were identified. To the later surprise of the Canadians, the rocks, some of them weighing many tons, weighed-in at the weight he had anticipated on his sketch, within a few kilograms. Furthermore, he next indicated whether the rocks were to be placed in the garden right-side up, or upside down, and his sketch of what he wanted matched the unseen undersides almost as though he had been able to turn them over before transport. His imagination was accurate, as though he had an intimate acquaintance with each of the rocks which would adorn the museum garden. Of course, there was no way that he could have moved them, but his intuitions about the underside of each rock were accurate without exception. My friend tells me that they are still talking about this feat at the museum.

The museum building itself is magnificent, made of yellowish-tan stone and designed in graceful curves, looking out over the Ottawa River and the Canadian Parliament buildings. The trucks were ordered to begin bringing the rocks to the museum site, and a crane was on-site to position each rock. The work began on a cold, rainy day, and as the sand and rocks were being positioned by the Japanese crew under Masuno's detailed instructions, the Canadian workers were surprised by the way in which the Japanese crew entered and left the actual site by walking in the footsteps of a single pathway, which had already been established in the mud on the site, rather than tracking mud all over the newly placed sand, or on or around the rocks, keeping tracking and foreign markings to a minimum. It was a degree of caring and concern for the state and cleanliness of the site that was itself quite foreign to the Canadians on hand.

Now completed, and a centerpiece of the museum for visitors, Masuno describes the garden as follows:

> It is called *Wakei No Niwa*, which, roughly translated, means to understand and respect all cultures—their history, spirit, and people—which leads to cultural

harmony. The garden design features an extensive gravel raked garden, a dry "waterfall," and a stone bridge. All materials used in this garden were selected in the hills surrounding the region. The dry waterfall is the focus of the garden and is the symbolic source of Japanese influence. . . . The dry stream wraps around the area, and appears to flow through the windows of the museum's Collections/Administration building, symbolizing the infusion of Japanese culture in Canadian culture. . . . It is crucial in building such a sparse design to listen to the "conversation" among all the materials—such as the plants and stones—as well as to be aware of the spaces between objects. Both the creator of a Zen garden and the viewer should be "at one" with the garden when they regard it. (Masuno 1999, 53–54)

Masuno's garden designs are "Zen-inspired," and he may be the only one at present attempting to create gardens which are patterned after the spirit of the great Zen gardens of the past. These gardens, which were built at the end of the fifteenth century and onward, were called "dry landscape" (*kare sansui*) gardens. Many of the old landscape gardens of earlier times lay in ruin after the Ōnin War (1467–1477), and rather than creating gardens in accordance with the aesthetic principles of beauty which had been in force, a simpler, austere, and probingly profound style of garden began to make use of the magnificent rocks which had been left behind after the massive destruction of the war. They were, for the most part, monochromatic, abstract depictions of the landscape paintings from China of the past. Craggy mountains, rushing waterfalls, river rapids crashing over huge riverbed rocks were all recreated in "dry" materials. At first, the designers were laborers, but within a relatively short time, the monks themselves took over the task: they were called "stone-laying monks" (*ishitatesō*). The gardens created are still termed "Zen gardens."

Masuno's Gardens

Masuno recalls that his early encounter with stone gardens began at about age sixteen, when his home temple garden was to be redone over a ten-year period. Katsuo Saito, a landscape designer of renown, was appointed to take on this task. Masuno's interest in academic study changed as a result of this undertaking, and rather than studying engineering, his academic course of study became design, including landscape design. While he attended university, Masuno worked under Katsuo during summers and holidays. After graduating, he became Katsuo's apprentice. He recounts what and how he learned from his master teacher:

> he never actually tried to positively teach design as such. Instead he would say, "First, work with the people on site" and "spend some time when the workmen are on a break, and consider thirty different ways in which to arrange a group of stones." . . . I . . . used to show him what I had done and asked him to comment on my designs. I would go away and think again before showing him the alterations that I had made. He used to say that however good the plans were, if I were not guided by the planting and layout of plants and did not actually go to see the plants and stones in situ, then I would never be able to come up with a good design. (Masuno 1995, 6)

Masuno adds that perhaps "the most important thing in executing a design is to talk to the plants and stones and hear what they themselves have to say about how they want to be laid out. In other words, I engage in a kind of dialogue with them" (Masuno 1995, 6). This theme of dialogue with rocks and plants constituted the most exciting aspect of the time I spent with him. It is not an easy matter to explain to a Western audience how it is possible to dialogue in this way. It is simply not part of the cultural traditions of the West. It has, however, a long history in Japan. Nishida Kitarō describes Japanese culture's most characteristic feature as moving from the subject to the object—object here refers to the environment, or any feature of the environment. And this movement from subject to object requires:

> negating the self and becoming the thing itself; becoming the thing itself to see; becoming the thing itself to act. To empty the self and see things, for the self to be immersed in things, "no-mindedness" [in Zen Buddhism] or effortless acceptance of the grace of Amida (*jinen-hōni*)

> [in True Pure Land teaching]—these, I believe, are the
> states we Japanese strongly yearn for. . . . The essence of
> the Japanese spirit must be to become one in things and
> in events. It is to become one at that primal point in
> which there is neither self nor others. (Tsunoda and
> Keene 1958, 362)

In his first major work, *Inquiry into the Good*, Nishida said
much the same: "To say that we know a thing simply means that
the self unites with it. When one sees a flower, the self has become the flower" (Nishida 1990, 77). This means that one must
"discard all of the self's subjective conjectures and thereby unite
with the basic nature of the flower. . . . Those without a self—
those who have extinguished the self—are the greatest" (Nishida
1990, 77). This does not mean, however, that a designed garden
results simply from uniting with the basic nature of a rock or a
plant. Rather, this uniting by emptying the self and becoming
one with a rock only describes what makes a genuine dialogue
with a rock possible. Then, one invests one's mind and heart in
the garden, and the result is an expression of the spirit of the person who created it, and who has become an integral part of it.
Whether or not the creator of the garden was spiritually enlightened, we can learn from the garden to the extent that the self-
cultivation of its creator has something to teach us through this
material and artistic expression of his or her spirit. If it is the
work of a true master of a craft, then that person must also be a
spiritual master, an enlightened being. Such a person, once having begun, becomes completely absorbed in the garden, its design, and its execution. "In other words, when the mind, hands,
body, time, and materials merge into one, then an unconscious
mind, which goes beyond the bounds of consciousness, is re-
sponsible for creating things" (Masuno 1995, 8). In this state, a
"perfect" or remarkable and lastingly memorable work of art
can be accomplished. Masuno believes that Zen makes possible
such states of awareness. It is Zen and meditation (*zazen*) that
leads many Japanese artists to a unity of conscious and unconscious minds, for "the conscious mind" is thereby able to find
"its way into the unconscious world. . . . *Zazen* or Zen meditation trains our consciousness and is the best way of reaching

down to the boundary between the conscious and unconscious mind" (Masuno 1995, 8). Readers of Nishida will recognize this state of spontaneous action united with immediate or direct knowing as "action-intuition." A martial artist responds to any and all situations without thinking; a Nō actor becomes the character and the gestures depicted; the *sumi-e* artist becomes one with the branch of the cherry tree which she is about to paint in a series of almost instantaneous strokes on rice paper which allows no hesitation or reconsideration; the tea master folds the ceremonial napkin without thinking, yet is fully aware, and wipes the tea bowl clean with a perfect and gentle motion. Virtuosity always appears effortless and graceful.

Nevertheless, even though mastery appears spontaneous and effortless, it is achieved through great effort, constant practice, and the unrelenting courage to continue. Masuno added that "the goal of Zen sitting is *satori*, or better, *kenshō*, which means seeing one's true nature, coming to know your true self and not merely the surface ego. But this real nature is invisible. Gardening is one way of showing oneself, of making one's nature visible via the various *dō*, including even poetry." As a member of the Sōtō Zen tradition, his placing of an emphasis on practice and not on achieving *satori* is central, for concentration on enlightenment can cause one to become oblivious to all that is worthwhile and important along the way to this one flash of awareness. So it is that in Sōtō Zen Buddhism the commitment is to practice, and it is the practice itself that is *satori*: it is not something which is elusive and far away, but it is right here now as practice. Practice is an expression of enlightenment itself, and not separate from some flash of intuition, which might or might not come, later on. Hence, in Sōtō Zen one just keeps practicing. And gardening, among the many *dō*, is one way of practicing and revealing one's nature visibly, if it is done mindfully.

The question is, then, how should one practice "mindfully"? Accepting that the garden is one's spiritual practice, Masuno always meditates before he begins. "I do standing Zen meditation for three or four minutes, at the site. This helps me to become peaceful, tranquil. Otherwise, with a racing mind, one would create a jumbled and out-of-control garden." One must empty his or her mind: "your *kokoro* must not be moving," but must be focused and as clear as a mirror-surfaced lake. Then, and only then can the "dialogue" take place. "When I encounter a stone or a tree, I communicate with it; I ask it where it wants to be planted or placed." In attempting to make this accessible to people who do not normally even imagine communicating with rocks and plants, he noted that "everything that exists has *busshō*—Buddha-nature—and every rock has movement, for me. It leads one left or right, upward or downward, and must be placed appropriately in order to create the right effect. So I ask the rock about itself." He ponders what angle will best draw out the character of the rock. Then, there is the relationship which a rock will have with all the other components of the garden. A garden is a relational space, and it is imperative that one consider the relational appropriateness of each element with all of the other elements of the garden. The central issue is "how to achieve *wa* [harmony] when two or more rocks are to be placed, given that one must now consider them in their own universe, the universe of the garden. In fact, a poorly designed garden is the result of the garden designer not having communicated with the rocks and the plants."

I and Thou

If everything that exists is a self-expression of the Buddha, or the universal, or God, or reality itself, then we have to grant that rocks and plants have the same status as human beings: everything is equally spiritual. Everything that exists is, simply, valuable in itself and for its own sake. Thus, "we must respect each other, sustain and preserve each other in a mutuality of help and assistance." Surely this is a fundamental starting point for any ecological ethics. "Everything that exists has *kokoro* (i.e., some sense of awareness): there is rock *kokoro*, and there is tree *kokoro*. In whatever form it exists, *kokoro* is to be respected. One must arrange the rocks or plants to express their own *kokoro*, and also arrange the rocks or plants in such a way as to express one's own philosophy and understanding. There is a mutuality of influence and effect. To do this is extremely difficult, for it demands a meeting of *kokoro* with *kokoro*."

Nishida Kitarō's most famous student, the late Nishitani Keiji, is one of the few philosophers to have struggled with what it means to dialogue with non-sentient beings. In his *Contemporary Problems and Religion* (Nishitani, translated manuscript in preparation), Nishitani utilizes Martin Buber's distinction, in *I and Thou*, between relating to people and things in a second and third person manner. One can relate to one's partner as a "you" or a "thou," or in the third person manner as an "it," a thing. Jean-Paul Sartre made a similar distinction between a person as *pour soi*, or *en soi*: as a self-conscious and introspective person, always becoming who he or she is, or as a static thing, which has no becoming, is relatively unchanged, unconscious, unreflective: such a person is like a rock. But Nishitani extends Buber's and Sartre's distinction to apply to non-sentient things as well as to human beings: he makes clear that a rock is more than an unchanging object, and not a being of lesser worth and interest than a sentient being. His account is as follows:

> a second-person oriented way of thinking is applicable to all manner of relations. I am sure that this way of thinking holds true not only of human beings, but also, for example, of animals. There are, in fact, ways through which those who keep a dog or a cat are related to these animals by calling them "you" or "thou," just as is the case with a farmer who is related to a cow or a horse by calling them by their names. This can be said not only of animals but also of a tree, grass, a stone or even such a thing as a desk. I think that there is something even in them concerning which we are able to relate ourselves to them as having the character of a "thou." . . . With regard to stones, Eastern people have long been accustomed to falling in love with them. While they love it, there takes place an exchange of communication between them. . . . To speak to a stone might sound like a metaphor, [but] . . . the question of whether speaking to a stone or to a plant is to be regarded as a mere metaphor or not is something worthy of deep contemplation." (Nishitani forthcoming, 66–67)

His analysis then takes him to an analysis of language, particularly as it relates to accomplishing communication with the non-sentient. The Greek *logos*, or "word," which comes from *legein*, which means "to gather," he relates to the Japanese *morotomo*, to be "together with." *Morotomo* is a relational indicator, indicating "that one thing and the other are together with each other. If this relationship can be described in terms of 'I and thou,' that is to say as *tomo* in Japanese, since this Japanese word also means 'a friend,' [then] what is here at issue is the friendly relationship between one thing and the other" (Nishitani in preparation, 68–69). Applying this to communication of the second person type with a stone, he concludes that "a human being and a stone are together, or stand face to face with each other. It is not the case here that these two things stand side by side in complete isolation. Instead, at a place where the relation of being between one thing and the other obtains, a deep connection is somewhere established" (Nishitani in preparation, 69). This connection, Nishitani contends, is the I-Thou relationship, the relationship of being genuinely together.

Furthermore, the ancient Chinese *dao* (Japanese *dō*), meant not only the "way" or "path" but also "to speak." Precisely what links these two very different meanings included in *dao*? Nishitani's answer is that the language in question is not the surface language, be it Chinese, Japanese, or English, which are always insufficient to say what needs to be said about relationship, love, and the "thou" of I and thou. Behind these surface languages, beyond the limits of spoken language, is the very source of language itself: "there is at the root of language a place which cannot be exhaustively expressed, but is rather that out of which language comes forth." Here *dao*, "path," and "to speak" are united into one. At this level, it is not so much that thoughts are exchanged through language, but rather "that one being bumps against the other . . . that one being and the other are together. . . . . A genuine togetherness can be established in the beings themselves, rather than through communication as understood in the ordinary sense." Indeed, we can say "that there are many cases in which we cannot communicate with each other through language but rather we understand each other without using language." For example, we cannot come up with the right words, and yet we can still understand each other, or we use the wrong words, and yet communication still exists. Lovers are very much aware of a communication that takes place without the use of words of any kind. Therefore, if there is communication without language, at that deeper level where language itself begins, then "the relation-ship of friendship is also capable of being established with a stone, with a tree or with a blade of grass and, in addition to them, with various kinds of animals." The relationship which one establishes with a particular stone means that it is not "counted merely as one of many stones." One's encounter with a rock oc-curs at that deep level, prior even to language, making possible a conversation without language where a feeling of kinship arises. The rock and I are in this world together, inextricably intercon-nected. We have always been in relationship.

Reviewing Masuno's relationship with the rocks and plants with which he engages, one finds the presence of this I-Thou re-lationship. He indicates that the degree of focus required to pull together the various elements into a coherent and harmonious landscape design is enormous. His description of the care which he takes in the initial selection of rocks is impressive: "Even when I am looking for suitable stones and other materials for a garden, I go up into the mountains and make numerous sketches in order to find stones and plants with the right degree of empathy." The term "empathy" is clearly a "thou" response: each rock and plant is unique, important, possessed of immense value, and to say all of this is already to be in an intimate relationship with the selected rocks and plants. The fact that such selection, as well as the on-site designing and positioning of the elements, is always preceded by meditation in order to put one in the right tranquil, receptive, egoless frame of mind implies a desire and willingness to be in relationship at a depth beneath language, at the level of *kokoro*. "I prepare my awareness by concentrating all my thoughts on my abdomen," the one point, the *hara*. The entire site is important, for the site itself has a history, and one must take this history seriously," he told me. "It is not acceptable to move in the earth-moving machines to fit some economic or leveling demand. The site, and its history, must be itself engaged as a part of the whole garden which is in the making." Therefore, "when I am on site, I don't simply arrange stones and things like waterfalls or cascades to suit the forms of the remaining concrete. Instead, what I try to do is to make the landscaping and such things as retaining con-crete walls fit in with the waterfalls, cascades, and other features that have been formed by the temporarily set out groups of stones, themselves arranged as a result of their dialogue with me."

He adds, "I wonder just what kind of spirit a certain stone has and how it would prefer to be set out. This is also true of plants and I always consider how I think the plants would like to be displayed. I always feel at one with the plants, when I am planting them and with the stones, when I am arranging them" (Masuno 1995, 10). To feel at one with plants and stones is, as Nishida argued, to become them, to reach their essence by letting them come to you. Both Nishida and Nishitani would understand Masuno's approach through "dialogue" with the various elements of the garden being designed and constructed.

The Ethics of Gardens

Having asked about his approach to garden design and construction, then I asked Masuno whether he would reflect directly upon the ethical implications of landscape design. Of course, the answer is well sketched by what has gone before, for it is all about the self-transformation which meditation and practice brings about for the practitioner. It is a *dō* of self-cultivation which, as a finished result, may also have the effect of bringing about transformation to some degree in the observers who engage the garden. In this sense, nearly everything discussed to this point is ethical in its import; from ecological respect and preservation, to the tranquility and peace of meditation, to the gift of gardening as social contribution for countless observers yet to come. Moreover, there were specific insights which he was eager to suggest.

Firstly, landscape gardening brings about a gentleness in the designer, the builders, and the caretakers. On this very point, I had the pleasure of interviewing one of the priests at the famous Saiho-ji temple, also known as Kokedera (the "moss garden"). This is one of Japan's most beautiful and overwhelming design creations, by Japan's most famous landscape designer, the Zen monk Musō Soseki (1275–1351). It contains more than one hundred different kinds of moss, creating a living carpet which extends to earth, trees, and rocks, and even to the ponds which are green with algae. The priest told me that the values which the garden teaches—the suchness or intrinsic value of each thing, connectedness, harmony, tranquility, and the sacred as the everyday, as something directly underfoot—had a direct effect even on the workers who themselves were not practicing Zen Buddhists. Nevertheless, they are transformed to a significant degree by the atmosphere of the garden; just to be in the garden on a regular basis has a remarkably transformative effect on all concerned. "Anyone can catch a glimpse of a higher spiritual awareness," said the priest, "and the garden is such an awareness offering insight into the worth of natural things, an atmosphere of peace and harmony, and the importance of community both among the workers, and with all those who quietly walk in its pathways."

The second value which Masuno listed is the developing of a respect for all things. Connected with the second, is the third, a diminishing of the ego, which leads to fourth, a robust sense of compassion for other people, and for all that exists. The fifth point is that landscape gardening also teaches that one must throw away one's concern about reputation and position, for one learns that these are unimportant. These are outward matters, and practice is about the inner, the invisible aspects of who one is. The garden is also a physical expression "of who I am to this point in my life."

Masuno told me that it is remarkably easy to see whether a student has designed just a so-so garden:

> One must ask whether one has been able to communicate with the stones. Does he respect the stones? Has he chosen the best position or placement for the stone's shape? Has the "space" in the garden been properly attended to? Is the overall atmosphere one of harmony, and yet a harmony which still possesses a robust tension (*kisei*). It is the tension between the garden's elements that creates energy. Is the composition of the parts such that a whole results? Is he afraid to leave spaces? Space is an important ingredient in a garden, for it points to emptiness, or nothingness (*mu*), and hence is fundamental.

The garden is an expression of "everything in me. But the garden is also my teacher, and I learn from it." The influence is double-sided, or one of mutuality. It is a spiritual matter, for "the garden is an expression of truth. All things are expressions of the absolute, of nothingness, of Buddha, and the garden is my expression of truth, respecting the radiating truth of each of the constituent elements. To realize that everything is an expression of self, and so everything is a manifestation of truth, makes one respect the *kokoro* of each thing." Ethically, "the garden teaches you how to live. Firstly, one is not alone, but always in relationship. I am always in relationship, as the components of the garden are always in relationship. Everything supports me (codependent origination), and so existence is a matter of mutual support." Ethics must take a "cosmic perspective," rather than a more limited perspective. Secondly, to live rightly is to preserve. Gardening, and appreciating a garden, bring cheerfulness: "one finds a flower blooming in an unexpected place, and one is gladdened. All that it takes is one, solitary flower. We come to appreciate the life of the flower—*inochi* [literally, mortal, or temporary life]—one respects the *inochi* of the flower." To practice a *dō* is to learn how to live one's life, for through flower arranging, gardening, or the martial arts, "we learn how to interrelate with other existing things." We learn what it means to be fully human, to practice "becoming the excellence of one's kind."

His final reflections were philosophical in nature, emphasizing that any of the *dō* teach us the sacredness of all things, for the sacred spreads out, well beyond the confines of a church, a temple, or a shrine. The physical expressions of the *dō* are extremely important, for beyond their importance as practice for the practitioner, they communicate by example. "The most important things cannot be expressed in words, and so the physical manifestations of the *dō* teach by example, rather than through abstract words—it is like pouring liquid from one cup to another." Plato, in his *Seventh Letter* (Plato 1964, 1589 [341d]), wrote that true insight is not communicated in words, but after long and continued interaction between teacher and student, quite suddenly a spark from the teacher ignites the mind of the student, and straightway nourishes itself." The teaching of ethics, for both Plato and the Japanese, is primarily taught by example, and the *dō* are centrally important in providing these examples. Indeed, they even create the possibility of examples by serving as the means for the development and growth of those who created them.

The garden raises one to a higher level: it is a taste of *satori*. It teaches that we must experience the flower directly and not through language, right now, in the living of one's life. *Ichigo, ichi-e*—"one time, one place" or "once in a lifetime"—the best time is right now, so plunge into it directly, and not abstractly or through the medium of language. Be in the moment. Masuno urged that "the garden is your own counterpart, and through it you can find yourself. It helps to make you more aware. It makes you ask, 'What am I?'"

To the extent to which one begins to gain insight into enlightenment, one becomes for the first time free to manipulate one's own mind: "this is radical freedom, for one now sees the connectedness of things, and that they are all empty, including the no-mindedness which is oneself, and so one is now free to choose which causes to remain involved in, which to leave behind, and which to seek out. One is now fully a cocreator in one's life. This is true freedom, and true mutuality. The universe is a constant influence on us, and now that we are free, we are a constant influence on the universe. Enlightenment is empowerment."

Previously, brief mention was made of the "moss garden" at Saiho-ji. The priest with whom I spoke echoed much of what Masuno has articulated. The moss garden is a representation or expression of nothingness. It teaches us the suchness of each thing, if one learns to interact with it directly, rather than abstractly through preexisting language and concepts. It teaches connectedness, harmony, tranquility, and the sacred as the everyday. "People come to the garden to experience these values, which they then carry over to their own relational situations. We are impelled to treat each other differently in the atmosphere of the garden. It is a 'holy' place, removed from the everyday, and yet what it teaches is how one is to live everyday." The Zen priest ended by pointing to a stone inscription at the entrance to the garden: *ichigo, ichi-e*, one occasion, one time. To be immersed in the garden is to have learned how to be immersed in the everydayness of one's life. There is always only the moment, and while the garden experience is just another moment, it is one which has drawn us into its essence, its magnificent harmony, tranquility, profundity, and interconnectedness. If we have experienced deeply, we will never be quite the same again, for we have been transformed, cultivated by the insights of the gardener's *satori*, and now, at least to some small degree, one lives one's life as though walking or meditating in a garden. One is thus engaged in practice, for one now tries to live one's life as though one were the gardener, which is surely the desired result. *Dō* means more than just a "path," but more importantly "the road of life," for one is now more free than ever to take over the designing of one's life. The landscape garden has taught what values are to be included in this life-designing, and how far one is to aim in moving toward the excellence of one's kind. The end result is a gentle affirmation of one's connection with all of existence, a sense of genuine relationship with rocks and ferns, trees and insects. To viscerally experience one's kinship with all of them is a giant step toward becoming an ethical person, one who works with the things which exist in order to create beauty, to offer a glimpse of truth, and to express goodness. To create is to cherish, to strive to preserve, and even to enhance our perception of the worth of that which is underfoot and all around us. The landscape garden, in all of its forms, encourages each of us to cherish and nurture this world of which we are an integral part.

CHAPTER FOUR

The Way of Tea (*Chadō*)—
To Live without Contrivance

The recently retired grandmaster of the Urasenke School of Tea, Sen Genshitsu XV, begins his book *Tea Life, Tea Mind* by recounting the brief exchange of a monk with his master: "'No matter what lies ahead, what is the Way?' The master quickly replied, 'The Way is your daily life'" (Sen 1979b, 11). As with each of the "Ways," the specific disciplines and techniques taught are meant to be generalized as habits for and in living all the other parts of one's life. Furthermore, these habits themselves cease to be habits and become internalized as spontaneous reactions to the varied happenings of everyday life. It is long and continued practice that leads to spontaneity, for in Japan, as I have said, spontaneity comes at the end of discipline and not before it. Discipline begins with the rote learning of specific techniques and principles, but it is not just that. Rather, discipline is a momentum toward one's own excellence, the self-cultivation of one's own being. The Way of Tea (*sadō, chadō, chanoyu*) is no exception. Learning to make tea is learning who you are. Learning who you are is to reconnect with the whole that each of us has been a part of all along. To make tea is an act of increasing spiritual awareness. It is also a magnificent expression of courteous and compassionate behavior toward others, and other things. Having observed the Way of Tea spread all over the world, Sen-sensei urged that "Tea teaches us how to approach the people around us, and how to get along with them." This heartfelt sensitivity to others rests on the understanding that our true selves are intrinsically good, intrinsically pure, and that each of us is a self-manifestation of the divine.

Background to the Way of Tea

The many influences which combined to help produce the Way of Tea include "the Shintō attention to purity and preference for pristine, natural materials; the Daoist view of the balance of *yin* and *yang* elements; the Confucian sense of propriety and social station; the sensitivity to seasonal references in *renga* (linked verse)[1] and, later, *haiku*—all have found their way into the conventions of *chanoyu*" (Hirota 1995, 27). Tea made its way to Japan from China, and it did so as an aesthetic practice and as medicine. As aesthetic practice, it was associated with courtly life, with finery which included art objects such as paintings, lacquerware, ceramics, fine fabrics, elegant furniture, fine metalware, and with poetry: "tea had already come to occupy a special place among cultured circles as a means by which they could transcend the mundane" (Sen 1998, 49). Dr. Sen suggests that this aestheticism in China found its way to Japan more or less intact: "for the Japanese upper classes tea was a unique and supreme device for abandoning the desires of reality and for building a world of freedom that transcended that reality. Tea at that time no doubt had about it an exotic flavor, and its rarity and its having come over from China greatly influenced attitudes toward it" (Sen 1998, 50). The drinking of tea carried with it extravagant social expectations. Dennis Hirota describes this as "lavish entertainment in a decorated hall," emphasizing that this heavily Chinese emphasis on the lavish gradually gave way in Japan to "*chanoyu* as a small gathering held specifically for sharing tea with formal procedures." He captures this dichotomy nicely: "a conflict or tension was experienced between the *shoin* display of Chinese art objects and the ideals associated with the thatched hut" (Hirota 1995, 35).

Tea was introduced into Japan as early as the late eighth century, and its first mention in Japanese literature appeared in 814 (Sen 1998, 47). Hoover reports that in 792, the Emperor held a large tea party for the elite, and for Buddhist monks (Hoover 1977, 172). It remained an aristocratic pleasure for several centuries, becoming popular in the twelfth century, thanks to its reintroduction by the famous Zen teacher, Eisai (1141–1215),

---

1. A *renga* poem is a form of *waka* running in a series, i.e., it is linked verse, composed by several persons, each striving to link both form and content with the lines that have already been contributed. A *waka* poem is thirty-one syllables and five lines. A haiku poem consists of three lines and seventeen syllables.

upon his return from a sojourn in China. Even then, however, while it was used in Zen monasteries in a ceremonial way, the aristocracy and warrior classes used it as a focus for elaborate parties. The interaction between the aristocratic and humble dimensions of tea continued, each influencing the other, until:

> Zen aesthetic theory gradually crept into the aristocratic tea parties, as taste turned away from the polished Sung ceramic cups toward ordinary pottery. This was the beginning of the tradition of deliberate understatement later to be so important in the Tea ceremony. Zen ideals took over the warrior tea parties. During his reign, Ashikaga[2] was persuaded by a famous monk aesthetician to construct a small room for drinking tea monastery-style. The mood in this room was all Zen, from the calligraphic scroll hanging in the *tokonoma* art alcove to the ceremonial flower arrangements and the single cup shared in a sober ritual. After this, those who would serve tea had first to study the tea rituals of the Zen monastery. (Hoover 1977, 174)

By the beginning of the sixteenth century, the lavish and ornate aspects of the Sung-style tea parties had been abandoned, and the simpler, more tranquil, natural, and rustic meditative enjoyment of tea had become the standard: "It was a genuine enjoyment of tea, even when made with ordinary or improvised utensils; an appreciation of the wonder of plain boiled water and the rugged surfaces of unglazed rural ceramics; a participation in hospitality free of contrivance and companionship free of calculation or pretense" (Hirota 1995, 35). This was the Way of Tea, although it remained for Sen no Rikyū (1522–1591)[3] to strictly codify its form, and to push the simplicity and rustic quality of art to its

---

2. Ashikaga Yoshimasa began building his Higashiyama villa and tea room in 1482.

3. He had been the favorite tea master of the *shōgun* Hideyoshi (1536–1598), when the priests at Daitoku-ji temple in Kyoto placed a statue of Rikyū atop its Mountain Gate in thanks for his contributions toward the gate's rebuilding. Rikyū's statue was clad in ordinary peasantlike straw sandals, and since Hideyoshi had to pass under the statue when entering the temple, he took offense at what seemed to him an act of prideful ego, and commanded Rikyū to commit ritual suicide (*seppuku*), which he did, at the age of 69.

extreme. Furthermore, the tendency to associate the Way of Tea with Buddhism, making it a spiritual or religious practice, had now become the norm. Serving and drinking tea became something more than just the adoration of beauty and human enjoyment, but rather had become a genuine "Way" to self-cultivation and the realization of one's own authentic nature in a world that was aesthetically, experientially, spiritually, and ethically transformed. This was *chadō*, the Way of Tea.

There were several "heroes" who were instrumental in taking *chadō* in this rustic and spiritual direction, with Murata Jukō (1421–1502) and Takeno Jōō (1502–1555) being central to this development. But it was Sen no Rikyū who, "by most accounts, even from the period of his own lifetime . . . brought the arc of development of *wabicha*[4] to its peak through religious conviction, keen sensibility, and intense creative activity. His student and fellow tea master Yamanoue Sōji would state repeatedly that Rikyū, in his sixties, had pressed his practice beyond the capacity of lesser teamen to imitate, declaring: 'Sōeki's [Rikyū's] *chanoyu* has already become a tree in winter.' . . . Not all modern schools of *chanoyu* trace their lineage to Rikyū, but even for those of the later *daimyō* style that draw directly on the traditions of Takeno Jōō, Rikyū remains a prominent figure" (Hirota 1995, 92). Nevertheless, a great many of the aesthetic ideals of *chadō* came from the *renga* poets, whose popularity was at its height as tea as a simple way of cultivation was emerging. "In a sense," writes Hirota, "the early founders of *wabicha* . . . were the genuine inheritors of a crucial element of the legacy of *renga*" (Hirota 1995, 37). *Wabi* was perhaps the central notion in *renga* poetry, and it became central to the Way of Tea as it is even today, and *wabi* remains the most important aesthetic notion in Japanese aesthetics, along with *sabi*.[5] *Renga* poetry, and the earlier *waka* poetry,

---

4. *Wabicha*, or tea *wabi*-style, refers to a complex aesthetic gestalt of qualities which will be described later in this chapter. As a guideline, *wabi* refers to the preference for the rustic, the natural, simplistic, frugal, humble, and the unpretentious, together with a touch of melancholy brought on by the recognition that the achingly beautiful before us, will soon wither and disappear. It includes recognition of the bittersweetness of the impermanence of all things.

5. *Sabi* refers to that which is never forced, never strained, ancient and yet graceful, as though revived from death. "Sabi," reflected Dr. Sen in my interview with him, "is like the pride of an old man making the effort to stand, while almost at death's door." A fine example of this concerns Ueshiba Morihei, who, "two days

was also referred to as *kadō*, the Way of Poetry. Yuasa describes what was required of a poet in this tradition: "the first step . . . is to have a very clear mind . . . by assuming the correct posture" (Yuasa 1987, 100). As with meditation generally, the hope is that enlightenment will come along with it. Yuasa writes that the highest state of *satori*:

> is the nondiscriminatory, compassionate mind that first thoroughly experiences and deals successfully with this transient world and then, from such a transcendent mental state, proceeds to feel compassion toward all sentient life. Similarly, the ultimate state for *waka* artistry is to attain such heights that one sees through this world's human afflictions and delusions, and yet, for that very reason, one is the mind of Great Compassion in the face of this world's delusory forms. This is a free mind that can empathize and share in the pain found in the various profiles of human life. (Yuasa 1987, 104)

Furthermore, quality *waka* or *renga* poetry must display *yūgen*, or profound mystery, for "such an ideal cannot be attained in a momentary conscious effort," but "if one undergoes a long period of training (*keiko*), forgetting the 'I' and immersing oneself in writing poetry, the way to artistry opens of itself" (Yuasa 1987, 100–01). This "training," however, includes a stilling of the mind through meditation, causing it to first become clear, rather than jumbled, and this is followed by a forgetting of the self and the appearance of spontaneous artistic insight. Buddhist training, as *keiko*, and artistic cultivation, as *shugyō*, merge. The Way of Poetry is a path to self-cultivation and *satori*, and such a state of mind and heart allows that freedom of being which can

---

before his death . . . raised his frail body to a sitting position . . . and indicated that he wanted to go to the bathroom. 'I'm sorry, but after lying in bed all day this old man's legs are very weak.' I quickly took one arm, and my close friend Yoshio Kuroiwa took the other. Slowly we proceeded down the hall, holding him tight lest he fall and injure himself. O-sensei suddenly straightened, pride flashing in his eyes. 'I don't need any help.' With a powerful shudder of his body, he freed his arms from our grasp. The weakened and dying old man had thrown two master instructors. Our bodies flew until we pounded into the walls on either side. Step by step Morihei Ueshiba made his way alone. With each step his life was burning like the last brilliant flare of a candle before its fire disappears" (Saotome 1993, 5).

then empathize and share in the pain found in the everyday lives of others. The meditative and aesthetic lead to the ethical or compassionate way of being in the world. They do not yield an ethics of rules and prohibitions, although these may well have been present earlier, but now one is able to operate out of a freedom to empathize with and to help others. Insofar as enlightenment includes realizing the oneness of all things, there would be no more reason to do harm to another being than there would be to do injury to oneself. In extreme or "desert island" examples where one is forced to do some harm to avoid a greater harm, the principle in place is to do as little harm as possible and, throughout, to be totally mindful of the aspirations and the suffering of others.

Wabi

Yuasa bases much of his analysis of the Way of Poetry on the writings of its major theorist, Shinkai (1406–1475), who was its most articulate exponent, and who was also a key figure in the analysis of *wabi*. Even for the Japanese, this remains an elusive and difficult term. To cite an instance, while serving as a visiting professor at the University of Hawaii, I arranged for a Tea ceremony to be performed for my students at the beautiful and authentic tea house nestled in a Japanese-style garden on campus. The tea house was brought from Japan piece by piece and reassembled by experienced craftsmen, maintaining its authentic rustic simplicity and beauty. At the end of the demonstration, performed by a seasoned tea master, someone asked the tea master if he could define *wabi*. He responded with a nostalgic and perplexed "aaahhh," thought for a period of time, and then said, "This is an extremely difficult notion to explain in words." And that was that. *Wabi* is a remarkably complex notion and, in addition, the master had just finished giving a demonstration of it through the ceremony, so we were all sitting in the midst of the *wabi* of the tea house. Yet it would have been misleading to point to the rough-hewn beams, the lack of nails or screws in the building's joinery, the pottery, the single flower in the *tokonoma* alcove, the sound of the iron kettle boiling, the simple acts of tea making and tea serving, the graceful movements of the master which seemed so spontaneous, and yet were so well-rehearsed, and so on. *Wabi* is none of these, for any one of these things could be contrived, or could appear contrived, which would not be *wabi*. Instead, it is a way of looking at the world and a way of acting in the world. *Wabi* stands for a highly complex aesthetic attitude, a way of seeing the world. In other words, *wabi* is an experiential whole, and not a mere collection of intellectual markers: to know *wabi* is to be in its midst; to have become *wabi* oneself.

A remarkable gloss on *wabi* and *sabi* is to be found in the retelling of an instance in Sen no Rikyū's life as a master of tea:

> Rikyū had a mind extremely sensitive to beauty from the point of view of *wabi* or *sabi*. He detected the smallest thing that went against it. When Rikyū was invited to a first winter tea party somewhere, he was accompanied by his son-in-law. When they stepped into the court, they noticed the gate hung with an ancient-looking door. The son-in-law remarked that it savored highly of *sabi*. But Rikyū smiled somewhat sarcastically: "This is far from savoring of *sabi*, my son; it is on the contrary a most expensive piece of work. Look here closely. Such a door as this is not to be found in this vicinity. It must have come from a remote mountain temple far away from the human world. Think of the amount of labor to bring it here, for which the master must have paid dearly. If he had understood what genuine *sabi* is, he would have searched for a suitable door ready-made or made to order among the neighboring dealers, and would have had it pieced together with an old board found about his premises. Then the door fixed here would certainly savor of *wabi*. The taste shown before us is not a genuine one." It was thus the son-in-law was taught the art in a practical way. (Suzuki 1959, 321)

Simply put, *wabi* is a way of seeing into the worth of things, a decided preference for the ordinary, rustic, simple, untouched, imperfect, old and withered, and as such, it is a way of seeing our usual world of luxury and brand names as an impoverished world of contrivance, empty reputation, and kitsch.

Wabi cannot be separated from Buddhist thought. It is related to awakening to the emptiness of self and world. The world as ordinarily seen, as object-full, is a fantasy created by the ego in an attempt to stabilize and solidify what is in reality everchanging and impermanent. Yet this very insight brings compassion to the fore, since the recognition that nothing exists separately and on its own means that it is interconnected with everything else in this flux of impermanence, and that everything and everyone is kindred in a sense far deeper than blood ties. Davey calls it an "aesthetic and spiritual concept" which tends to "evoke a perception of beauty in the fragile, impermanent nature of life and suggests that genuine beauty depends on this very impermanence" (Davey 2003, 103). Furthermore, the fleeting quality of life, and existence generally, creates a sense of melancholy, of sadness, even to the edge of despair, for the beauty of the world, together with the joys of the world, are transitory and always already disintegrating and decaying. Our recognition of impermanence carries with it a sadness; and yet, awareness of impermanence also carries with it an intensified sense of the preciousness of each moment and each of the things of this world. Davey catches this insight well when he writes, "the universal impermanence in life" results in a recognition "that relationships, even those we cherish, are fleeting. They exist in the moment, and once this is seen with our whole heart, every moment becomes precious, stretching beyond the boundaries of time" (Davey 2003, 81–82). In this sense, melancholy is not mere sadness, but a recognition that in an impermanent cosmos, the beauty of the moment is raised to a high aesthetic crescendo; *mono no aware* is a phrase which incorporates the sadness of melancholy, and the exquisiteness of each and every detail of life. Summer is so very short; the leaves will soon turn to color, and then these too will fade, dry, and fall to the earth, leaving only bare branches nourished by the now-decaying leaves lying all around the tree's trunk. My children, too, are such a source of exquisite delight, but now they are beginning to grey, encountering some of the hazards of living. I am well into my "senior" phase, aware that the "end" that once seemed so far away is now so much closer. All of this is *wabi*, but there is much more. For this melancholy, at the edge of despair at times, is also absolutely joy-filled, for the fleetingness of an impermanent reality simply renders each and every moment a vitally precious moment. *Ichigo, ichi-e*—one time, one place—for there will never be a moment exactly like this one ever again. As cherry blossoms last for an hour, a day, or a week, so our lives are bordered by uncertainty and the potential devastation of life's storms and dangers. Yet this only makes each moment all the more wonderful, even as it is precarious, or rather, precisely because it is precarious, mysterious, and unknown. Make tea as though this was your last opportunity to celebrate with others in this deliciously intimate way. Take hold of the mystery of each person and of each object in the tea hut, for all has come from nothing and will return to nothing. As Suzuki writes, "poverty, *sabi* or *wabi*, simplification, aloneness, and cognate ideas make up the most conspicuous and characteristic features of Japanese art and culture. All these emanate from one central perception of the truth of Zen, which is 'the One is the Many and the Many is the One,' or better, 'the One remaining as one in the Many individually and collectively" (Suzuki 1959, 27–28).

Yūgen, or "deep profundity," is laced with the incredible mystery that something exists, even if impermanently, rather than nothing at all existing, and so is to be treasured just as it is. Eliot Deutsch, who wrote the foreword to this book, has amplified the meaning of *yūgen* in Japanese aesthetics as that which lies beneath the surface, and he introduces an interesting contrast: "*yūgen* is at once entirely natural and wholly spiritual" (Deutsch 1975, 31). Furthermore, he underscores the importance of art when he writes that "the concept of *yūgen* teaches us that in aesthetic experience it is not that "I see the work of art," but that by "seeing the I is transformed" (Deutsch 1975, 32). He concludes that it is not that artworks possess the property of beauty, but that beauty is the artwork itself: "beauty, then, is not so much a quality of a thing as it is the thing itself as a presence to be apprehended in loving joy" (Deutsch 1975, 34). Surface beauty turns out to be a shallow account of the aesthetic, spiritual, and transformative worth of anything: it is nothing more than surface glitter, likely short-term delight, and little more than entertainment. Art with depth, however, is more than surface glitter, for it bespeaks the eternity which is its background and which "lines" the foreground; it is profound in that it veils a wisdom and insight from which we can learn something more each time we return to it for additional nourishment and understanding. Rather than being entertainment, it is an aspect of the self-cultivation of the artist which, if we are open to his or her message, will also transform us and lead us to a higher sense of possibility than we might have otherwise realized.

The "just as it is" of *wabi* is important. A discerning person will not need glitter, or awareness of cost, or a reminder of the fame of the craftsman who made the object. Hamada Shoji, perhaps the world's most respected potter of the twentieth century (and the subject of chapter 6), did not sign his work, just as most ancient craftsmen did not sign their pottery, for if it is quality work it is recognizable and not at all in need of further identification. A deeper perception sees profound beauty in the ordinary, the plain, the unpretentious, the austere, the worn, the weathered, the old, the withered and faded, and the imperfect, rather than in the complete, static, and rigid deadness of symmetry. Hirota, following the *renga* theorist Shinkai, refers to "chill" as implying "simplicity, lack of adornment, and austere tone," meager, uncontrived, sparse, rough, ordinary: these are *wabi*, and they represent an embrace of the ordinary as seen in a new light (Hirota 1995, 51). The "chill" spoken of here refers to the perceptual change that occurs when the self "falls away," and "the ordinary things of the natural world disclose a beauty pervaded by a profound sense of pathos and mystery" (Hirota 1995, 40). The falling away of self dissolves the "dichotomous perception of things as objects standing apart from the self" (Hirota 1995, 42).

Wabi also means to cut through reputation, ego, economic status, and power as human pretense. The door to a tea house is just big enough to crawl through. It is too small to carry worldly goods or weapons inside; it reduces everyone to the same physical stature, pointing to the equality of everyone in their basic natures. Each of us is already divine, just as we are, if we would only let it shine through the clutter of self-centered civilization. All are equal in the tea hut, and this equality allows a new compassion to be shown. For "in the world of *wabi*, ordinary things manifest themselves anew and with trueheartedness are seen as though for the first time" (Hirota 1995, 92).

It was Rikyū who brought the sense of *wabi* to its most refined simplicity and ordinariness. Plain, rough *raku* pottery (his innovation) "adopted the sandy clays and low-temperature firing methods used in rooftop tiles to produce teabowls. Simple in

shape and bearing black or reddish glazes without ornamenta-
tion, these bowls were highly functional, with broad bottoms for
kneading the tea, and bodies that insulated its heat, while pos-
sessing an austere beauty" (Hirota 1995, 94). Rikyū also preferred common bamboo for flower containers and tea scoops,
and plain wood waste containers: "in *shoin* style tea, such containers had usually been bronze, while Takeno Jōō used ceramic
ware" (Hirota 1995, 94). It was Rikyū who minimized to the
fullest extent possible the size of the crawl-in door, and reduced
the tea room size to the smallest possible. He also adopted the
single bowl for thick tea which was passed to each participant.
Rikyū left no written record, and even the famous One-Page Testament, which, while sometimes attributed to him, was almost
certainly not actually composed by Rikyū. The One-Page Testament appeared within ten years after his death (Hirota 1995,
242–43). His teachings, like the teachings of Shintō, were simply
picked-up through oral teaching, internalized through practice
and perfected by observing the graceful practice of one more advanced. Rikyū's single page of instruction is said to have been
written from a Pure Land Buddhist perspective, and yet most
commentators have stressed that "tea is Zen."

Zen and Pure Land

Tea practice evolved as a religious practice under Zen's influence.
Two documents, *Nampōroku* and the *Zen Tea Record*, make this
relationship clear. The latter makes a distinction between ordinary or worldly tea and "Zen tea." Hirota summarizes the teachings of the *Zen Tea Record* on this point: "true tea is Zen tea:
true because it leads its practitioners to awakening, and because it
is itself the emergence of true reality, in the Buddhist sense, in the
lives and acts of tea people" (Hirota 1995, 97). This work begins
by affirming an isomorphic relationship between Tea and Zen,
starting with the phrase "tea of no guest, no host." Buddhism
teaches that there is no substantial self, and recognition of this
yields a tea event which includes no host and no guests. Ordinary
thinking makes a sharp distinction between self and others, and
self and things. With the "dropping off" of the ego-self, nothing
is separate from anything else, and the distinction between subject
and object is no longer operative. A tea gathering, as a result, no

longer objectifies, but rather, as Nishitani and Buber have made plain, is an event of a "Thou" interacting intimately with other "Thous." The designation "thou" does not identify distinct and separate others, but rather suggests the merging with and becoming the other. The *Zen Tea Record* states that "if you are to take up the teascoop, immerse your heart and mind fully in it alone and give no thought whatever to other matters" (Hirota 1995, 265). One finds one's own original nature in the tea utensils, for everything is a self-manifestation of the One. A practiced and sensitive practitioner will experience the "*samādhi*[6] of handling utensils," indicating that the acts of tea are themselves acts of meditation, and as such are revelatory. The sustained focus required is the signature of the seasoned meditator:

> When, in putting down a utensil, you release it and withdraw your hand, do so without in the slightest dismissing it from your awareness and shift the mind just as it is to the next utensil to be treated. Prepare tea as the forms (*kata*) prescribe, without relaxing the spirit at any point; this is called "performing in the continuity of spirit." It is wholly the functioning of *chanoyu-samādhi*. (Hirota 1995, 265)

This is a description of the *samādhi* of a mind that is single and undivided, clear and serene, tranquil and relaxed. If Tea is practiced as a meditative act, we are told, then there will be clear ethical results as well: "If you apply this attitude without any lapse in both the activity and the stillness of daily life, then without any laboring in deliberation all matters will be well disposed; the proper relationships of lord and vassal, parent and child, and person and person will spontaneously reach perfect fulfillment" (Hirota 1995, 268). The relationships indicated are, of course, the cardinal relationships of Confucianism, which were taken over as the primary ethical teachings of Japan as well. Virtue will spontaneously appear when one has become a good person, a

---

6. *Samādhi* here refers to total concentration. The term is used in connection with the practice of meditation, and refers to fixing attention on a single object, which is also a method of discouraging discursive thinking.

person of *jen* (human-heartedness) in Confucian terms. Furthermore, if one steadfastly observes the "spirit of *wabi*," then one will not become miserly, or transgress the teachings of Buddhism, nor give way to anger or avoidance, or become slovenly, or foolish. Instead, these "will be transformed into charity, transgression of precepts into observance, anger into perseverance and humility, slovenliness into energy, confusion into meditation, and foolishness into wisdom" (Hirota 1995, 275). Instead of striving to do what is good, one has become a good person. One may be said to have reached the "other shore" of enlightenment. The ethical requirements of Buddhism are now no longer separate from oneself, and one lives a spontaneously compassionate life, beyond rules. Rules no longer apply, for they were but stepping stones, hundred-foot poles with which to vault to a higher place, or rafts to self-realization taking one across a body of water to the other shore. Now that one has landed firmly on that other shore, and with a unified mind and heart embodying the moral ideals, one can improvise and apply the moral precepts in new and unusual ways as circumstances demand and permit: "there are rules, and yet there are none" (Hirota 1995, 276). This is not to say that one can now live in ways that flaunt the rules, but rather that one now operates effortlessly from that insight or place which produced the rules in the first place.

In Tea, as in ethics, one must first become one with the rules and procedures before one can go beyond them. One is then a master in the true sense. One can now manifest "one's own intent" (Hirota 1995, 285). Rikyū did just that by simplifying the Way of Tea, and in doing so he broke many rules and bent the Tea tradition out of its conventional shape. He helped to create a practice which has endured for nearly five hundred years since his death, codifying the meaning and essence of what constitutes *wabi* in Tea and, as a result, ensuring that the Way of Tea would rank as an important "way" to self-cultivation and enlightenment in Japanese culture. "Tea is about *satori*," I was told often, "and nothing less than *satori*." The practice of Tea, when undertaken with "total exertion," is itself *satori*.

Yet there are also the Shin or Pure Land Buddhist influences on Tea to be taken into consideration, for the One-Page Testament seems to draw on Hōnen's (1133–1212) One-Page Testament (*Ichimai Kishōmon*). Hōnen opened the Pure Land tradition to everyone, even the illiterate and the sinful, on the grounds that the compassion of Amida Buddha is infinitely available to each and every person, however poor or confused she or he may be. What distinguishes Pure Land from other schools of Buddhism, and from Zen Buddhism in particular, is its single-minded reliance on other-power (*tariki*), rather than self-power (*jiriki*). D. T. Suzuki summarizes this difference by means of an analogy: defenders of other-power as most important adopt a "cat" theory of enlightenment, or salvation. A kitten is carried to safety by the mother cat alone, who grabs it by the scruff of the neck, whisking it away from danger. There is nothing for the kittens to do but to "let their mother carry them." Self-power, by contrast, offers a "monkey" theory of enlightenment or salvation: "baby monkeys grasp their mother's body with their limbs or tails, so the mother is not doing the work alone. The baby monkeys do their part. The cat's way is monadism, for the mother alone does the work. The monkey's way is synergism, for two work together" (Suzuki 1970, 65). Simply to call upon or to recite the name of Amida Buddha—*namu-amida-butsu*—elicits the grace of Amida Buddha, because of the Buddha's compassionate vow to save all sentient beings. It is not because of the supplicant's sustained efforts, or good works, or merit that enlightenment is achieved, for each of us is finite, weak, sinful, and unworthy. It is by the grace of Amida alone that enlightenment is attained. There were periods in Pure Land history when the "expert authorities" insisted that enlightenment would be granted only if the *nembutsu* was said in a certain way, or with a certain mindset. Hōnen rejected all such niceties, for only the action of the Buddha is operative here. Hōnen wrote of *suki*, the devotion to one's art and its mastery, as the operative principle in art, which eventually allowed deviation from tradition in order to enhance its relevance to later generations. In the One-Page Testament, *suki* is used to mean considerably more than dedication to one's art and its mastery, for the Way of Tea is seen as an art "motivated and informed by a compassion for things and for one's fellows. In the love termed *suki*, artistic and religious aspirations are one . . . this love takes as its model the compassion of the Buddha" (Hirota 1995, 110). It is not that this ethical dimension is missing from Pure Land, but that by the time of Rikyū it became a central aspect of *suki*'s meaning. One must follow the Buddha in eliminating the attachments of ordinary life, and in so doing one abandons the self-centered perspective. One becomes no-self, making possible the emergence of "no host and no guests." In one sense, one is cut off from this world, becoming an exile so to speak, and yet in another sense one is now planted in the world as though for the very first time. The often quoted refrain that "first I saw the mountains, and then I saw that there were no mountains, and then, finally, I saw the mountains again," but now transformed by the new and profound awareness of the nature of reality, is apt here. But from the Pure Land perspective, such enlightened awareness is a gift of Amida Buddha, requiring nothing for its achievement. Similarly, the One-Page Testament asserts that the Way of Tea is "simply to drink tea, knowing that if you just heat the water, your thirst is certain to be quenched. Nothing else is involved" (Hirota 1995, 245). And the thirst in question is much more than the desire for a cup of tea. It is the thirst for transformation, for seeing into one's nature, and into the true nature of reality, for enlightenment itself. To satisfy this thirst, just make tea. But now making tea has become a matter of "ultimate concern" involving other "friends" and a variety of "objects," each of which has been rendered precious and unique. Like St. Francis of Assisi, but in the expanded Japanese context, one caresses "brother spoon," and rejoices at the gentle, bubbling sound of "sister kettle." The transformation which occurs is one which renders each and every thing, each and every one, a "thou," and the resultant obligations—spontaneously occurring obligations—are to cherish and preserve their being, and to create an environment in which to open the possibility of transformation and insight for all those present. This could be the moment for the gift of enlightenment, where all present lose their everyday egos in order to find their true selves, or if they are like-minded achievers, then the moment is even more delicious because all are together focused on the delicate wonder that is this moment, in this place, and with these kindred spirits. It is truly an exquisite moment in which one is in love with the entire universe: "When one has cast off all clinging, one's love reaches out beyond the bonds of the self so that no barriers of possessiveness or calculative thinking stands between subject and object . . . [this results in] encounters with others that are free of all designing" (Hirota 1995, 111). One has become pure in heart, for, as Rikyū allegedly remarked in the tiny document attributed to him, "know that when you simply cleanse your heart and mind, all things essential are inherent in that." The Way of Tea is to "simply heat the water with wholeness of heart" (Hirota 1995, 245).

From Sen no Rikyū to Sen Genshitsu XV

The recently retired fifteenth-generation *Iemoto*, or Tea Grandmaster of the Urasenke school, Dr. Sen Genshitsu XV, has done much to make *chadō* available to an audience extending worldwide. He is an outstanding ambassador for peace for the United Nations, as President of the United Nations Association of Japan: "I have toured the world for more than a quarter of a century with the goal 'Peace through sharing a bowl of tea.' The simple act of serving tea and receiving it with gratitude is the basis for a way of life called *Chadō*, the Way of Tea" (Sen 1979, front cover).

"Tea is a way of communicating," he began his interview with me in the conference room of the Urasenke school, in Kyoto. "Tea is *kokoro* to *kokoro*," from heart and mind to heart and mind, soul to soul, depth to depth, thou to thou. This way of being with others "is contagious, for as the host attends meticulously to the feelings of his guests, then everyone else begins to attend to the feelings of the other guests." It is this quality, Dr. Sen urged, that gives Tea such an important role to play in the development of world peace. Such results can only be attained through practice, but the aim of such practice has a decidedly ethical content: "the guests will 'feel' what the host intended to 'give' them in and through the ceremony. An intense level of kindness prevails, and the guests learn through this enveloping atmosphere to be kind to one another in turn." Moreover, "the Way of Tea is a way of meditation, and through it one learns how to become more attentive to the feelings of others." Once again, learning to be kind is not just the intellectual recognition of what kindness is, but through mind and body as unified, one actually practices being kind. This principle is driven home over and over again in *aikidō*. For example, the instructor said to us on numerous occasions and in different ways, "Don't just sit there thinking 'this person is going to fall.' You have to act, to unite body and mind by reaching out and keeping the person from falling. It is not just a thought process: it is an actual doing as reaching-out with your body to help." It requires practice, and not just on one or two occasions, but whenever an opportunity to be kind presents itself. A kind person is a person who habitually performs kind acts, and one who may occasionally be seen to actively seek out opportunities to be kind as an expression of his or her own inner, developing nature. Hosting guests in the tea room demands such kindness through insisting that this one occasion be as perfect as possible for the guests. What would they like? How can they receive the utmost pleasure, and the utmost insight into the deeper truths of the practice of Tea? What can be done, however insignificant it may seem, to assist each guest in their continued self-transformation and development?

Tea is a way of meditation, but to do it properly, "one must eliminate preconceptions. One must start from emptiness, from nothingness (*mu*). It is necessary to purify your heart in order to reach the *mu* state. And the host is himself attempting to reach the *mu* state while serving the guests tea." The serving of tea is a form, a *kata*, which anyone can understand, and anyone can practice. It is radically accessible, but the goal is not the imitation of the form, but "to become *one* with the form. In fact, when grasped from the inside of experience, the form begins to look at you. The Japanese word *michi*, which means 'the way,' can refer to the form becoming one with you." He went on to explain that in the martial arts, when you become one with the form, you can anticipate the moves of your opponent. The way to develop this oneness with form is by using your failures to lead you along the way. Dr. Sen then said something surprising about his own practice: "After fifty years of continual practice, it has been only very recently that I have settled into a oneness with the form." Practice is never ending, but it is sometimes imperative to remember that the practice of a Way is indeed a lifelong practice. Dr. Sen told a charming story to fix this point even more strongly. He recalled that as a boy, his father used to tell him that one must continue to practice Tea even after one dies. "I found this incomprehensible at the time, and thought my father a little strange. But now I understand the truth of what my father taught me. The Way of Tea is never ending."

Furyu

As we dialogued on a sunny early October day, the tall cedars
outside were gently waving in the breeze. Every branch was in
motion, and the trees were swaying back and forth, glistening in
the bright sunlight as they did so, creating ever shifting patterns
of light and shadow. Dr. Sen pointed to the unceasing motion
visible through the room's large windows, saying that like the
breeze and the branches, the Way of Tea "follows nature's path:
it is a flowing which is not obvious." It is called *furyu*. *Fu* means
"wind," and *ryu* means "to flow": "this suggests that our spirit
should flow through life like the wind that flows through all of
nature" (Sen 1979, 66). Such an approach allows one to appreciate nature, and life, in their changeability, enjoying winter as
winter, spring as spring, and all the stages of life as worthwhile
in themselves. It is not that one does not desire coolness in the
heat of summer, but while accepting that summer is hot, there
are many subtle ways to suggest coolness in one's living, and in
serving tea: "in Zen, when you become one with the cold or heat,
the extremes of hot and cold disappear" (Sen 1979, 68). Eliminate preconceptions and prejudices, and become one with ever-
changing nature. The result, is joy in the moment: "you become
so impressed by everything around you that you could die. You
become open to the subtle, continual and ever-present changes
all around you. Flowering and dying, summer and autumn, and
one's feelings about all of this are a part of the meanings of *wabi*
and *sabi*." *Mono no aware*, the sadness yet appreciation that is
related to the fact that the flowers that are now budding will also
soon wither. It is a sadness tinged by joy, joy tinged by sadness.

The Lineage

A direct descendent of Sen no Rikyū, Dr. Sen was the fifteenth
Grand Tea Master of the Urasenke school before handing the
headship to his son. Rikyū was the first Tea Master of the
Urasenke school, and Rikyū's son, Shōan (1546–1614), the second. Shōan's grandson, Sōtan (1578–1658), succeeded him, and
three of Sōtan's sons each established a separate school of "Sen-
family Tea," viz., Urasenke, Omotesenke, and Mushanokōjisenke.
All three claim their inspiration from Rikyū in particular.

If, as Dr. Sen suggests, living a life patterned after the Way of Tea is to live without contrivance, then the simplicity of this was captured by Rikyū in seven principles: (1) make a satisfactory bowl of tea, (2) lay the charcoal so that the water boils efficiently, (3) provide a sense of coolness in summer and warmth in winter, (4) arrange flowers as though they were still growing in the field, (5) be ready ahead of time—do not rush, (6) be prepared in case of rain, (7) act with the utmost consideration for your guests. These seven rules are, of course, deceptively simple. Principle number six, for example, implies that while anyone can make tea in the sunshine, that is, when conditions are ideal, it takes a master to make tea when it rains. True mastery in practice is, while encountering new situations, dealing with any difficulties which might arise with an ease and spontaneity which displays, at the same time, imperturbability. This holds for everything that one does: "The principles of the Way of Tea are directed toward all of one's existence, not just to the part that takes place in the tearoom. In practice, the test lies in meeting each occurrence of each day with a clear mind, in a composed state. In a sense, even one's smallest action is the Way of Tea" (Sen 1979, 11).

Rikyū emphasized harmony, respect, purity, and tranquility as the central principles, or "virtues," of Tea. "Harmony" is expressed in the interaction of the host and guest, the food served, and the utensils used with the flowing rhythms of nature. "Respect" refers to "the sincerity of heart that liberates us for an open relationship with the immediate environment, our fellow human beings, and nature, while recognizing the innate dignity of each." To further this point, in our conversation Dr. Sen emphasized that everyone is a divine manifestation of the universal whole. "Purity" is important to Tea, as it is to both Shintō and Buddhism, and includes not only the preparation for the tea gathering and the serving of food and tea but also the cleaning-up and the storing away of the utensils afterward. Such actions as clearing the dust from the room and the dead leaves from the garden path all represent cleaning the "dust of the world," or the worldly attachments, from one's heart and mind. "It is then, after putting aside material concerns, that people and things can be perceived in their truest state. Finally," continued Dr. Sen, "'tranquility' is achieved by practicing the first three principles."

Furthermore, "this tranquility will deepen even further when another person enters the microcosm of the tearoom and joins the host in contemplation over a bowl of tea" (Sen 1979, 13–14).

Beyond Language

All of the Japanese ways are beyond words in the sense that they are experiential practices and not theoretical or intellectual activities. In *aikidō*, landscape design, or Tea, it is absolutely necessary to get the "feel" of the art and its so-called principles. "In Tea, one reaches beyond words," said Dr. Sen. I inquired whether he meant that there is a pre-linguistic "place" or depth out of which language itself emerges. Nishitani speaks of such a place, as did his teacher, Nishida, who emphasized "pure experience" as the raw material, the "given" out of which we carve concepts and words. Dr. Sen agreed, for Tea practice leads back to the pre-linguistic and pre-conceptual, and eventually becomes a pure expression of that which is beyond, before, or beneath language. This is what it means to become one with the form (*kata*) of Tea: "one reaches a point where it is now *chadō* that is practicing people, rather than people practicing *chadō*." One achieves this through practice, attempting to eliminate all boundaries between host and guest, self and act; to become one. "Tea is very different from a performance, which is why we call it the 'Way of Tea,' and not the 'Tea ceremony.' A performance or ceremony implies a gap between the performer on stage, and the audience. In Tea the goal is to eliminate the gap completely." It is a communal act, and if successful, each participant lifts the others to a higher state of awareness, a higher level of kindness and appreciation where everyone is not only of equal rank, but of no rank whatsoever. In the tranquil, harmonious, and rustically beautiful atmosphere of the tea hut, one is encouraged to meet others at an intrinsic level, rather than at an outer or extrinsic level: one meets the other as a thou. The kindness and harmony experienced in the tea hut points to what we can become, after crawling back out of the hut and into the outside world of everyday cares. If it is possible to carry the peace, tranquility, sensitivity to beauty, and the kindness and respect learned into the world, then *chadō* will have contributed significantly to mutual understanding, and to world peace, which Dr. Sen has worked so tirelessly to assist. Tea is a pathway to self-transformation, including the positive transformation of relations, of communities, and the interactions of human beings with each other, and with the world. It is a particular instantiation of the greater way of the universe itself. It is to become one with the Way, through the specificity of a "way."

Zhuangzi, the fourth-century BC Daoist philosopher, wrote metaphorically about the limits of language and the superiority of a direct communication beyond words:

> The fish trap exists because of the fish; once you've gotten the fish, you can forget the trap. The rabbit snare exists because of the rabbit; once you've gotten the rabbit, you can forget the snare. Words exist because of meaning; once you've gotten the meaning, you can forget the words. Where can I find a man who has forgotten words so I can have a word with him. (Chuang Tzu [Zhuangzi] 1964, 140)

Had Zhuangzi and a tea master met on their wanderings, one could imagine them sitting across from one another by an open fire, taking tea together and smiling contentedly at the wordless conversation in which they were engaged. It is the meaning beyond the words that one has somehow to catch, for the words themselves are nothing more than fingers pointing at a reality which can only be known in the marrow of one's bones.

CHAPTER FIVE

The Way of Flowers (*Ikebana*)— Eternity Is in the Moment

Introduction

The Way of Tea was a major stimulus in the development of the Way of Flowers. Tea was also important to the development of other arts, e.g., pottery, *sumi-e* painting, and calligraphy, as represented in the *tokonoma* (a recessed alcove), that culturally important alcove found in homes, and even in office buildings, and, of course, in the tea room. The influence of tea on these other arts can be discerned even today in most Japanese homes. Even today they usually include at least one "Japanese-style" room with a *tokonoma*, which regularly features a scroll (either an appropriate example of *sumi-e* ink painting or a calligraphic rendering), a pottery vase, and some sort of simple, yet exquisitely presented flower arrangement, each tailored to the season or to a special event. The tea room, too, always includes a *tokonoma* in which the tea master presents a scroll or painting, a piece of pottery, and a subtle floral display selected to depict the chosen theme of the day and always in collective harmony. Each of these arts encouraged the other related arts, but it was the Way of Tea, remaining incredibly popular over hundreds of years, that did the most to help keep them in the forefront of awareness. The Way of Tea employed the other arts to achieve an aesthetic experience of subtle intensity that it sought, and yet each art has since become a way or practice of its own, while remaining vitally important to the Way of Tea as well. This is especially true of *ikebana* (literally, "arranging flowers"), the Way of Flowers.

The importance of flowers has been traced all the way back to the Buddha himself. On one occasion, when his disciples had gathered on the slope of the Mount of the Vulture to hear the Buddha's sermon, the Buddha mystified the assembled crowd by not uttering a single word. Instead, he simply held up a flower— some say a bunch or bouquet of flowers—and all fell silent, expecting his words to follow. But he said nothing more: there was no sermon, although this turning point in Buddhist history has come to be called the flower sermon. It was a turning point because it is now thought of as the beginning of Zen Buddhism, the wordless or direct transmission of the enlightenment of the Buddha, to his disciple Kāshyapa,[1] who alone understood what the offering of the flower signified. We are led to believe that to everyone else, the gesture resulted only in confusion and disappointment. But this one disciple understood what the Buddha was communicating, and he smiled. This story, whether true or apocryphal, represents the heart of Zen, for it is a communication based not on oral teachings or scripture, but on a direct and immediate wordless transmission. You either get it, or you don't. That the Buddha chose a flower to hold up may well have been incidental. Perhaps it was simply at hand, and it could have been a stick, a stone, or a bird's feather. But, in fact, it was a flower, and the fact that it was a flower has helped to fix the story in the minds of succeeding generations. For most of us, flowers are memorable, accessibly beautiful, universally pleasing, and dynamically and colorfully present.

What the Buddha eventually said, after seeing Kāshyapa's smile, was that "the eye of the true *Dharma*, the wonderful Mind of *Nirvāna*, the true formless Form, the mysterious Gate of the *Dharma*, which rests not upon words and letters, and a special transmission outside the scriptures; this I hand over to the great Kāshyapa" (Dumoulin 1979, 16). Handed on to Kāshyapa was both the flower and the mantle of leadership, for he came to be recognized as the second patriarch of Zen Buddhism, with the Buddha being the first. The way to the truth of things can be found in a flower, or in anything and everything else, for all things are revelations, self-manifestations of the universal originating creative energy.

---

1. Kāshyapa, or Mahākāshyapa, was one of the more prominent disciples of the Buddha. He became a teacher and preacher of renown.

Stella Coe, who was an eminent flower master, reminds us that *ikebana* should be understood to mean "Japanese flower arrangement," for it is "the art of arranging more than flowers" (Coe 1984, 18). Coe suggests that a literal translation of *ikebana* is "living plant material arrangement," and "the flowers are generally the least important part of the arrangement" (Coe 1984, 18), although the "art of living flower arrangement" might be closer to the literal meaning, understanding that the prefix *ike*, which means "living," carries the demand that the arranger do what is required to make the arranged flowers look as though they were still alive, as they would be found in nature. Twigs, branches, stems, fungi, leaves, bark, and other plant material may be included in an arrangement. However, as central as the materials used and the principles of effective arrangement are, "how you go about it will require a different way of thinking about flowers and arranging them." Elaborating on this difference, Coe writes:

> Western arrangements tend to favour a mass of flowers, full-blown flowers playing the predominant part and the combination of colors having the greatest importance. The Japanese approach is just the opposite. You might almost say that the Japanese rule of thumb is: the fewer flowers the better. The full-blown flower, the half-open bud and the tight bud may be used to symbolize past, present and future. The Japanese emphasize the significance of the whole of a flower or branch, its life cycle, so to speak; what you see in a single flower, or any other piece of plant material you may use, can epitomize the eternal processes of the universe. (Coe 1984, 18)

As with all the Japanese arts, the key to success is practice (*shugyō*), and the results of the practice include an increase in physical and mental well-being, a deepened respect for nature as well as for one's fellow men and women, a markedly diminished ego, together with the growth of a spiritual dimension, "a tranquil attitude and an abiding gentleness of character. These attributes will come out in your arrangements quite naturally, as through your practice they become part of your own nature" (Coe 1984, 126). The arrangement itself is just a pointer, a symbol indicating the depths and magnitude of what lies beneath the surface: the flower arrangement itself is an expression of and a pointer to the developing profundity of the psychological, spiritual, aesthetic, and ethical self-development of the artist-practitioner. Yet what is being revealed is not something added onto or mixed in with who one once was. Rather, practice merely reveals what has been there all along, from the beginning, but was covered over by the accretions of wrong-thinking and ego-centeredness. Practice brings to the surface who you really are, and "your basic nature, your real self, underneath layers of conditioning, will rise to the surface. And they will be apparent in all of your other activities, your words, thoughts, and feelings as well" (Coe 1984, 126).

Zen and *Ikebana*

Zen Buddhism spread far beyond the samurai warriors, and its influence on Japan has been enormous, most notably in Japanese aesthetics, as we have already discovered. But it is with flower arranging that this sense of aesthetics spread to nearly all social and economic classes in Japan. The utensils used in tea can be expensive and scarce, and few can afford the money or the space for a tea garden and tea hut, but anyone can pick plant material or buy it cheaply. One writer, reporting on the state of affairs during the early part of the twentieth century, remarked that nearly every woman in Japan had at least some exposure to *ikebana*.

Ikebana usually traces its beginnings back to a line of Buddhist priests called Ikenobo—meaning "a simple hut beside a pond"—which began with Ono no Imoko, a seventh-century court noble who retired to the priesthood. Inspired by his visits to China, he built his own landscape garden, more or less patterned after the ones he had visited, but in usual Japanese fashion, adapted it to the Japanese environment. He took particular exception to the haphazardly arranged offerings of flowers placed on Buddhist altars of worship. He spent his last years developing the art of flower arrangement, attempting to work out its principles and forms. Coe summarizes his deeper aims:

> The task he set himself was typically Japanese in its paradoxical nature. He was trying to find a way to cut the flower (or branch) from its native stem, thereby shortening its life, and then find a way of placing it in water in order to prolong its life. But he went further

than that. As a Buddhist priest he felt that an arrangement placed before an image of the Buddha should symbolize the whole universe. From the beginning in a humble hut beside a pond—*ike-no-bo*—came the style known as *rikka*, "standing up plant cuttings." For hundreds of years the techniques were passed from master to master, usually priests. (Coe 1984, 23)

Ikenobo

The most outstanding artist and systematizer in the Ikenobo lineage was the fifteenth-century Buddhist priest Ikenobo Senkei. His fame as a flower artist spread widely and many would-be followers made their way to his temple, Rokkakudo, in Kyoto, which stands to this day next to the metal, stone, and glass office tower which is the Ikenobo headquarters.[2] There are dozens of distinct schools of *ikebana*, each with its own style, but Ikenobo remains the standard in the field, although not the only one.

I had the pleasure of interviewing several people, including a master teacher of flower arrangement of twenty-years, while at the Ikenobo school of flower arranging. Miura-sensei, the international teacher at that school, confirmed that "one's whole life will be expressed through one's arrangements. The goal is *satori*, of course, but many other aspects of one's personality and character change along the way, as well." One learns to respect the flowers, and even the clippings. She spoke of one student, a young boy, who fell in love with plants: "he arrived at Ikenobo with intelligence, and he left with *kokoro*, as well. The changes in students are subtle, yet obvious. They become less boisterous, much more respectful, more able to express themselves, and in control of their emotions. There is an increase in happiness, in self-esteem, and in sheer enjoyment of life."

As Masuno communicated with the rocks, so too Miura emphasized that students learn "to talk to the flowers in a very short time." Sugihara Seiha, a professor of *ikebana* at Ikenobo

---

2 Rokkakudo Temple was built in 587, under the auspices of the beloved Prince Shōtoku, Prince Regent for Empress Suiko. Shōtoku was the author of the Seventeen-article Constitution, which is still taken as the primary document in the founding of Japan and the Japanese spirit.

headquarters, in a demonstration at the Japan Foundation in Toronto, remarked that in his arrangements, "the flowers just wanted to be arranged this way. I am just listening to the dictates of the flowers."

I asked Miura-sensei if *satori*, in relation to flower arranging, meant a glimpse of or grasp of the emptiness of all things, and with it, a recognition of the interconnection of all things in the fullness of the pure experience of the moment. Without hesitation she replied, "exactly so." She then added, "in fact, when the students themselves become empty, they do very well at *ikebana*. Everything is empty, interconnected, and sacred." She also agreed that the sense of the oneness or divinity-in-all-things is the bedrock of ethics and emphasized that one needed to be in a state of internal harmony, and needed as well to interact harmoniously with one's environment, and in one's arrangements, in order to continue to grow and develop either in life, or in *ikebana*.

Shintō and *Ikebana*

Central as Buddhism was to the development of interest in flowers and their arrangement, Shintō, too, must be given its place. Older than Buddhism in Japan, Shintō is, in essence, reverence for all of nature and for all natural things. Everything that exists may attract or actually be *kami*. Recall that *kami*-nature refers to the awesome or mysterious, the "aha" moments in life. Surely everyone includes flowers as being high on the list of things awesome and breathtaking in their experience of the world. Flowers dominate festivals, weddings, funerals, special days, special events, openings of shops, schools, government buildings, and airports. Shintō teaches a reverence for nature, and one can see its influence in the tender way in which the materials for flower arrangements are handled, which extends in detail even to how trimmings are to be disposed of. They must be carefully and neatly rearranged for disposal, carefully wrapped, tied into neat bundles, bowed to and thanked, then gently and respectfully placed in the trash container. To do less would be to dishonor the flowers, nature, the divine, and oneself. Yet a paradox still lurks at the base of this respect and honor heartfully displayed: one has cut the very flowers that one strives so diligently to honor. One has killed the flowers, disturbed the natural cycle, and shortened their lives.

The *Kōan* of Living by Dying
and Dying by Living

Perhaps the most insightful response to this *kōan* of cutting flowers to preserve living flowers, was given by Nishitani Keiji, whom we have discussed before. To respond to a *kōan* is the most that one can do, for by design a *kōan* is a puzzle that is insoluble, a paradox that cannot be resolved rationally, and a question for which there is no logical, discursive answer. To ask what is the sound of one hand clapping is to ask a question which admits to no rational answer. Any "answer" will have to be a non-rational one. One might shout, or twist the master's ear, or break into dance, or hold up a flower. To do so is to respond in some way which is other than, or beyond, the rational. Yet the response also points back to the question, revealing the limitations of using the rational intellect for dealing with many life issues, and directing attention to the importance of immediate and direct experience, to an authentic taking-in of the question in order to react with the whole of one's being. Just now, right here, on this unique occasion, one is oneself the answer to the question. At this moment, here, now, one is completely and fully the answer to this or any other possible question. To live and to act with a robustness and determination which approaches joyful intoxication, while suspended in the space-time moment, book-ended by the nothingness prior to one's existence and the nothingness that ever looms as the threat of one's own death, is a vital and visceral response to our "existential situation." Of course, to merely mimic the aforementioned responses would yield no experience of resolution, leaving one no further ahead on the path to enlightenment than one had been previously.

Nishitani, in his brief article "The Japanese Art of Arranged Flowers" (Nishitani 1995, 23–27),[3] begins by recalling a newspaper story about Jean-Paul Sartre's interest in *ikebana*, an unexpected interest for an atheistic French existentialist. The story did not give the reasons for Sartre's interest, but Nishitani attempts to supply them, based on his own reaction to *ikebana* upon returning to Japan after having studied in Europe for two and a half years. He recalls that he returned to Japan with new

---

3. Since Nishitani's article is less than five pages long, references to page numbers will be few.

eyes, "with something of a foreigner's understanding." He mused that the great cathedrals of Europe were meant to last, as though forever, and the museums were fortresses which safely housed and preserved art treasures into the indefinite future. *Ikebana*, by contrast, "is created to last only for a short time." It moves with, and is created to be in accordance with, the ever changing seasons: "it is, by its very nature, something temporary and improvised." Such arrangements are vivid and vital responses to the *kōan* of living while dying, and dying by living. To live is to use up one's life, to bring one's life another step closer to death, simply by living in time. And the explicit transiency of a specific arrangement only serves to highlight the incandescent brilliance and energy which it expresses. What is to be found in the interval between death and death, or more precisely between nonexistence and death, is a life lived vigorously, purposefully, and mindfully, as, for example, in a heroic act of self-sacrifice or the intense love of another. "The essential beauty lies precisely in its being transitory and timely," appearing "out of the impermanence of time itself. People who arrange flowers understand this." In this sense, *ikebana* is the perfect art of Buddhism: it faithfully depicts the impermanency of all things, and the sheer emptiness of all things. The cut flowers of *ikebana* are already dying, and yet like the rest of us, they die by living with zest and exquisite beauty. Of course, we do not all live this way, but if one lives "authentically," to use Sartre's language, then one greets each and every moment as one's defining moment, the moment that says to the world, "yes, I am here, and this is who I am for this is what I do." It is to make oneself by doing, by acting in the world and engaging others. The flowers are already dying, as we are, and yet it is against this immanent background that they are at their brightest and best. So, too, can we live our lives, our dying.

Nishitani suggests that what distinguishes *ikebana* is the cutting of the flowers and branches. Unlike gardening, which grows and nourishes plants and flowers in order to preserve them, *ikebana* cuts branches and flowers from their roots, knowing that to do so is to kill them, in the very short run. This, too, is an enactment of a Buddhist theme, for garden plants embed their roots into the soil in such a way as to resist being dislocated, or pulled out of the earth. This resistance represents a will-to-live, a struggle to survive, "as if it [the plant] were trying to get ahead of time, continually going beyond itself, forging ahead of itself." Time is not to be denied, nor can one somehow "beat" it: the persistent plant "is fighting a losing battle with itself." To look at it in this way, the plant is being inauthentic by not facing the fact that it will die, that it is vulnerable, impermanent, and subject to decay and decomposition. But cut flowers make no pretense: they are dying right now, and dissolution and decay have already begun. There is no pretense, no struggle against the inevitable, and certainly no attempt to transcend time. The time cut flowers have is short, and the only option available is to make the best of it, to make their short-term living an interval of exquisite beauty and robustness. The meaning of "timeless" has now become an interval of robust intensity, of shimmering delight, of unfathomable beauty which is so perfect and so fully engaged that, once having been, it can never be lost. This interval is inscribed on the face of time itself. It does not attempt to deny time, but lives precisely in the face of time's incessant passing. As Zen master Dōgen might have said in response, time flies without flying, and passes without passing. Nishitani takes the analogy of plants and trees and applies it to the living of life as a human being:

> And not only trees and grass, but people as well—all natural life is so. Plato said that all living things seek eternity in this changing world through procreation, but even here we can find the same attempt to deny time while in the midst of it. The life of the artist and his urge to produce . . . is the same as the life of natural things. Art belongs to the world of man and his culture, and is different from simple nature. But life in art has its fundamental source in the life of nature. . . . *Ikebana* is a severing of this very life of nature. Flowers in the field or garden pollinate in order to procreate. This is part of the natural will or desire of life. The arranged flower had this will or desire cut off. It is rather in the world of death, poised in death. It has become severed from the life which denies time, and has itself entered time and become momentary. (Nishitani 1995, 25)

Already in the world of death, cut off from its life and without any further need to deny time by pretending to be permanent and immortal, it is now fully in time, having become authentically momentary. A cut flower does not "conceal" the fact that it is a temporal being, by inauthentically parading itself as permanent, substantial, and eternal: "the flower with its roots cut off has, in one stroke, returned to its original essential fate in time." By being cut, the flower reveals its essential nature—like a response to an unspoken *kōan*, itself designed to call upon us to reveal who we really are, rather than who we think we are or ought to be, rather than recite what other people and social institutions say we are and ought to be—as empty, a fleeting series of moments flashing bright, or dull, as we choose, against a background of nothingness. The flower is what it is, and likewise we are all rootless branches and flowers in our essential natures. We are empty, fleeting moments in time. Like cut flowers, we, too, are rootless in that we are without a substantial self and exist for a relatively short time against the background of nothingness, to which we inevitably return.

Yet in another way, Nishitani suggests, the rootless flower has transcended time; it has been cut off from the constructs of time that occur in life, and it is just as though it stands in the timeless present. The "timeless" is redefined as not referring to eternity, for continued "substantial" existence is a far-off world of hope and imagination, but the momentary, the here and now, which is eternally present, "a momentary point in which there is no arising or perishing." This, then, is a fuller answer to the *kōan*: live life with "total exertion," as Dōgen taught, act by act, encounter by encounter, moment by fulsome moment. Just as Dōgen urged that to begin to meditate with "total exertion" is already to be enlightened, for enlightenment is not some far-off event removed from the practice here and now, so ethical living is not some far-off catechism or standard to be applied but is to be found in the everyday and underfoot. To be ethical is to act selflessly (for one is empty, rootless), with compassion (with total engagement since being ego-less, or at least less ego-full, is to be the universe and is actually to be the "other"), and right here and now (*ichigo, ichi-e*). Like a flower, each of us is an eternity in each and every moment of time. Eternity is to be found precisely in the now. To come to realize this is to be transformed on the spot, for transformation involves understanding who one really is and to be compassionately related to existence in its fullness. The realization is to know oneself to be eternity within time, and not as just a being who is slowly withering and decaying. It is to live as though severed from the constraints and rigidities of time, suspended in an emptiness which is timeless. The result is an emptiness that is a fullness, of potential and bright possibility, moment by precious moment. One is now able to live in a carefree and ecstatically joyful way, suspended in an ocean of infinite possibility and, therefore, creative novelty for as many moments as one has ahead.

Reflecting on the *tokonoma* as the space that flower arrangements have traditionally been allotted, Nishitani writes that "within that space, the flowers exist with solemnity, floating in emptiness, just as though they have emerged from nothingness." Each moment is a new birth, a new opportunity for a transformation resulting in a new and more striking way of looking at oneself, others, and the world at large. The flowers in the *tokonoma* electrify the entire room, just as a single individual entering a room can make his or her presence felt intensely without uttering a word. What presents itself is charisma, *ki* energy, radical authenticity, compassionate goodness, and they are uncontrollably contagious. Jealousy, hatred, and negative thoughts can block them. Of course, neither the flowers, nor the person entering a crowded room, intend to have that effect. Miura-san, of Ikenobo, remarked that "even a single flower, if placed just right, can take control of a great hall, or of an entire space." The person and the flowers "are simply there, in their correctness," and, it might well be added, "in their concreteness." The effect is the result of a nonverbal communication, like the Buddha and his wordless flower sermon, which communicates that which is both priceless and possible, timeless and eternal in the form of the momentary, with only a smile or a gesture exchanged. What is revealed in the nothingness at the depths of the flower or person is *yūgen*, or profound mystery and great depth. *Yūgen* is akin to Nishida's lining of the *kimono*, which is unseen, and yet seen in the way a garment "hangs," and so it is invisible yet visible, imperceptible yet striking. The recognition of the profound in the depths of the everyday is a reminder of eternity in time. Thus, "finitude itself, in being thoroughly finite, represents the eternity behind it. Time itself, in being completely temporal, becomes an eternal moment. With the activity of cutting, emptiness is unveiled in the depths of existence, and the eternal moment is realized" (Nishitani 1995, 26). The flower is the divine incarnate, the divine made flesh or material. *Ikebana*, like tea and the other *dō*, unveils "eternity by being thoroughly temporal." It arises not out of the will to live, or the desire for the permanency of soul, or the false immortality of progeny or reputation. Stripped down to its essential nature, it just is, but what it is, is a creative embodiment of the divine, a sacred trust to be cherished but not clung to, to be sustained but not embalmed, and above all to be delighted in right now, in this place. The flower lives without willfulness, is expressive of its nature just as it is, and does not pretend to be everlasting. Like a shout, or the tweak of a nose, or a spontaneously kind act, it just is!

Reflections of a Pioneer

During the 1920s, Gustie Herrigel, while living in Japan with her husband, Eugen Herrigel (author of the classic *Zen in the Art of Archery*), became the student of Master Takeda Bokuyo, who instructed her in *ikebana* over a period of several years. Her account of these years, as told in *Zen in the Art of Flower Arrangement*, is a passionate and insightful description of *ikebana* as a spiritual path, told with considerable philosophic understanding. In preparation for her first lesson, at her home, where all subsequent lessons took place, Takeda-sensei sent ahead all of the materials and tools that would be required. The lesson began with the unwrapping of the plant materials, which was not mere preparation, but a modeling of the proper attitude required: "Carefully the bast that held the bundle together was untied, without using the shears. No pulling or cutting, no impatience, no disorder. The bast was carefully rolled round the finger and laid on a table. Everything was done in a timeless silence, every move of the hand was executed precisely and soundlessly. Concentration on the real work had already begun" (Herrigel 1987, 6). The handling of the plants, even at the preparatory stage, was understood to be as vital an aspect of flower arranging as the clean-up and the proper disposal of the cuttings at the end. Here was teaching by example, the aim of which was not just to teach techniques and basic skills, but to convey attitudes which would apply both to flower arranging and to living one's life generally. The aim of the Way of Flowers was to assist in bringing about an inner transformation which would then be evident in one's every subsequent act, and this inner transformation would even be evident in the arrangements themselves.

Continuing his wordless teaching by example, the master struck a contemplative or meditative stance before beginning to carry out the actual arrangement design:

> Now follows a contemplative examination of the loose branches. Each one is lovingly examined and tested for its pliability and natural "bent." . . . Much depends on your being able to feel how the branch accommodates itself most willingly, thus entering into a relationship of inner tension with it. . . . One might think the plant must suffer no pain, so carefully is it handled, until it finally keeps the desired form. (Herrigel 1987, 7–8)

This first lesson, typical of those that followed as well, "passed almost wordlessly," for emphasis is placed "on communication 'from heart to heart.' It was thought that only through personal transmission could the spirit of the teaching be protected from dogmatic rigidity" (Herrigel 1987, 11 and 15). A comparable approach in the West was advocated by Plato, if one reads him as an open-ended thinker and teacher, as I do. Plato guarded against the dogmatic rigidity of teaching and learning by leaving his dialogues unresolved, having presented the several sides of the issue under consideration with considerable force, and then suggesting that the participants should meet again soon to continue the discussion. He insisted that the point of his teaching was to bring students to see for themselves, which also was the aim of his teacher, the great Socrates, rather than to have students memorize principles, or to accept solutions on his authority. The Buddha, too, warned his students not to accept anything that he or anyone said simply because he had said it, but rather to try it out for themselves, in their lives, in order to determine whether it rings true in the living of their lives. Plato, in his *Seventh Letter*, counseled that true learning was ultimately a wordless event which passed from teacher to student:

One statement . . . I can make in regard to all who have written or who may write with a claim to knowledge of the subjects to which I devote myself—no matter how they pretend to have acquired it, whether from my instruction or from others or by their own discovery. Such writers can in my opinion have no real acquaintance with the subject. I certainly have composed no work in regard to it, nor shall I ever do so in future, for there is no way of putting it in words like other studies. Acquaintance with it must come rather after a long period of attendance on instruction in the subject itself and of close companionship, when, suddenly, like a blaze kindled by a leaping spark, it is generated in the soul and at once becomes self-sustaining. (Plato 1964, 1589 [341b–e])

Herrigel's account differs from Plato's in that the method of teaching is wordless, rather than dialogical, but for both "the first requisite . . . was a spiritual affinity between the two [teacher and student], and above all the proven ability of the pupil to grasp his Master's teaching intuitively" (Herrigel 1987, 15). She remarks that communication from heart to heart includes "the hidden intention of not simply letting the pupil learn a definite body of doctrine by rote, of not handing on to him ready-made knowledge and clever tricks, but of arousing in him the duty of discovering the spirit of flower arrangement through his own experience" (Herrigel 1987, 16). What is being conveyed is a comprehensive approach, and not just a scattered attitude or two; it is a way of living one's life as a spiritual undertaking. She writes that:

If he [the student] wants to penetrate to its roots, he will be forced to decide whether he was attracted only by the artistic and aesthetic elements, or whether he seeks to experience the all-embracing, total nature of this art. In the latter case he will have to admit, again and again, that he must begin like a child, that any sort of ambition is a hindrance, and that any desire for personal uniqueness stands in the way of development. That, quite small and modest, he must look away from the ego in order to work as quietly and selflessly as this Eastern attitude demands. (Herrigel 1987, 22)

The truth is that what one is being taught is how to live one's life through the sustained practice of this particular aesthetic form, such that "the performance itself is of secondary importance compared with the inner attitude" (Herrigel 1987, 23). And even though one learns by imitating the teacher, the ultimate goal is not imitation, "but bit by bit he begins to realize, and perhaps also to experience, that this 'fitting in' is actually a springboard for true creativity." Herrigel confirms that the advanced student will never rest content with mere copying. Rather, insights gained by observing become a vital part of the "slow inward transformation and maturation," which only sustained and committed practice (*shugyō*), over a lifetime can bring (Herrigel 1987, 30–31).

The Principle of Three

The philosophical foundation of *ikebana* is the Principle of Three, which divides the universe into three realms which, in their depth, are at the same time one: heaven, the earth, and human beings. It is a depiction of the order of the cosmos, and this order is repeated in the inner nature of a human being: the microcosm imitates the macrocosm. The longest stem, or branch, represents heaven, the shortest earth, and the stem or branch of intermediate length represents human beings. Human beings occupy a mediating position between heaven and earth, as participants in the heavenly or formless realm and in the material or earthly realm of forms. In *aikidō* one strives to act in accordance with the laws of the universe. In *ikebana*, too, only by acting in accordance with nature can one's creative powers fully develop and express themselves. One must learn to flow with nature and its laws, rather than to strive to overcome them, to conquer nature. When one reaches the highest levels of accomplishment, one is so settled into the Way of Flowers that one's actions have become spontaneous and seemingly effortless. As Davey confirms, "one finally observes a flower in a state of such heightened awareness that no distinction exists between the observer and the observed. And in that instant, one realizes the essence of existence in a single petal poised between life and death" (Davey and Kameoka 2000, 31). In this state of mindfulness, the rules are you, and you naturally express them in your creativity, which includes and yet reaches beyond them:

> The Principle of Three contains, in its unsymmetrical structure, the reciprocal action of fullness and emptiness, vitality and detachment; it encloses the whole cycle within it. In his work, the pupil gives the totality of heaven, man and earth a further 'unfolding' in visible unity and symbolic form. He implants into it the limitations of his ego and at the same time equalizes them. Since he participates with his whole being, the little ego becomes unimportant in the total cosmos; it makes way for the non-ego. The European from his standpoint might formulate this as follows: after the differentiations are surpassed, the way to one's real self is unfolded, and hence to wholeness. The pupil will then cling to the pattern no longer; he will forget the Principle of Three. It ceases to exist; the stepping-stones are forgotten so as to reach the everlasting origin. (Herrigel 1987, 38–39)

It is clear that what the *ikebana* teacher teaches by his conduct is that "the pupil's human dignity, uprightness, tact, and responsibility is as important and meaningful as the learning he [the teacher] imparts" (Herrigel 1987, 46). Toward this end, there is, after all, a written aid, referred to as the "Book of Rules," which underscores the importance of the development of the entire individual. In it, the student is asked not to "chatter" in class; not to pretend to know more than she or he knows, not to be puffed up, for there are many stages of awareness and advancement to be gained beyond the current stage; to achieve a "delicacy of feeling," to handle flowers delicately; and to speak kindly of the other schools, while abandoning anything inferior in one's own school. These are attitudes that one is urged to develop. Consonant with these exhortations to the student, there are "ten virtues" which the teacher should embody: these include bringing all aspects of *ikebana* into spiritual relationship, uniting the hearts of the flowers with the human heart, and both of these with the universal heart "in this sacral and indescribable atmosphere that animates the room in which pupil and Master come together for a common task" (Herrigel 1987, 72). Herrigel glosses this account when she states that:

> Intimately connected with the flower heart is the universal heart—the relationship with people. Yet all are equally important and equally justified. There is no preferred realm, say the realm of man and of human things, as if he were the crown of creation. There is not even a clearly delimited realm of life; for the Japanese all life is an uninterrupted unity, springing from a common root. If he distinguishes plants from animals and both from men, he nevertheless does not believe in differences of value, as though one were higher than the other, more important and more valuable in the meaning and purpose of being. It may well be that a flower or a branch of blossom reflects the pattern of life more purely than the man who deems himself an exceptional phenomenon. (Herrigel 1987, 72–73)

This "sacral atmosphere" is such that "it is as though people could not behave meanly in the presence of flowers, and as though their nature were refined by having to do with them" (Herrigel 1987, 74).

Other virtues for the teacher to exemplify include being free of cares, i.e., a capacity to accept with equanimity whatever fate has in store; showing one's "love and esteem of all human beings"; the obligation to create a classroom atmosphere filled with "harmony and reverence"; presenting the unity of body and soul in one's teaching and doing; and displaying humility and reserve in dealing with others (Herrigel 1987, 65–69). The virtues are many, but they all point to the importance of creating a sensitivity in the student toward his or her surroundings, relationships with other human beings, and with the world of nature as a whole. This is the way of "right behavior."

A Culture of Flowers

Anyone who has visited Japan knows that throngs of people flock to the seasonal viewings of flowers (*o'hana-mi*), and the list of such occasions is surprisingly long: plum blossoms, cherry blossoms, iris viewing, hydrangeas, wisteria, lotus blossoms, cosmos and chrysanthemums and, of course, autumn foliage. This is not a complete list by any means, but it does represent the festival viewings which I actually attended during my time in Japan. During one of my visits, I arrived in Tokyo during cherry blossom viewing time. At the noon hour, the streets and pathways, parks and temple grounds where the trees were, were thick with people. One simply shuffled along, by necessity, in step with the many. In front of me, two bedridden patients from a nearby hospital were being wheeled along—still in bed, smiling as they went—their intravenous bags and tubes waving in the gentle breeze. They were smiling with delight at being in the midst of the crowds, under the cherry blossoms which were so thick and full that the entire atmosphere was colored pink. The nurses who were pushing them were also smiling broadly, caught up in the drama of this magnificent display. In this communal event people were somehow united by the sheer marvel of a springtime bursting into the world of form all at once. Cherry blossoms (*sakura*) are a powerful symbol of the Japanese acceptance of change and adaptability, for the blossoms will be gone in a week at most, and far sooner if there is a storm or a strong wind. As a symbol of the transient and momentary, these blossoms teach the importance of immersing oneself in the now, fully engaging in the beauty and wonder of those things which are momentary, and relearning that each and every occasion is an occasion of intrinsic value, for each breaks through the mystery of existence itself, into the forms of the momentary. Festivals reconfirm the sacredness of the momentary as the form of eternity, of the many as one, and the vital preciousness of just being alive in the world, with others. Herrigel writes that "the Eternal itself is immediately present in its living beauty" on such occasions. She adds that the purpose of the arts in Japan is to convey the sense of harmony, for "harmony is the innermost form underlying nature, life and the world" (Herrigel 1987, 91). What is revealed through art, festivals, and ceremonies is that which cannot be expressed or represented, the eternal itself—absolute nothingness (*mu*). And yet while these arts express the inexpressible, they remain art, while revealing a harmony of heaven, human beings, and the earth. The arts in Japan come closest to giving voice to the voiceless, and form to the formless. Art accomplishes this by directing attention to the particular and finding in each cicada, each stone, each flower, blade of grass, and dewdrop an intimation of the eternity which lines each and every thing in this world, if one would only makes the effort to read nature, to merge with nature, and to instantiate the Buddhist vision of the interconnectedness of all things. In this sense, art takes over where philosophy and ethics can never go.

CHAPTER SIX

The Way of Pottery—
Beauty Is in the Abdomen

Introduction

The intense appreciation of flowers by the Japanese is equalled only by their love of pottery. And while pottery is not designated as a *dō*, it has often been treated as one in Japan. Hamada Shoji (1894–1978), whom many acknowledge to have been one of the greatest potters of the twentieth century, was appointed a Living National Treasure, Japan's highest honor in the arts. His colleague and friend, Yanagi Sōetsu (1889–1961), with whom he was involved in the development of the folk art movement, remarked that the love of pottery "is almost universal" among the Japanese, in large part because of *sadō*: "Tea taught people to look at and handle utilitarian objects more carefully than they had before, and it inspired in them a deeper interest and greater respect for those objects" (Yanagi 1972, 148), that is, at the level of highest artistry. Yet the highest level of artistry has less to do with technique and more to do with the "heart." However, what the term "heart" signifies may be far more than one might expect. Yanagi points out that "handcrafts . . . maintain by their very nature a direct link with the human heart, so that the work always partakes of a human quality" (Yanagi 1972, 107). He contrasts handmade crafts with machine-made items which are inevitably "children of the brain," rather than of the heart. Hamada agreed with this account, speaking of the "heart behind the hands" (Leach 1975, 20). He was thoroughly trained in the technical, the chemical side of pottery, but quality pottery does not arise out of either technical know-how alone or intellectual

117

brilliance. Quality art arises from the heart, from one's capacity to feel. The point he wished to make was that quality art arises from the body's ability to feel, or, on the basis of the notion of bodymind unity, then from the unity of both body and mind, both feeling and knowing how to express these feelings in clay. Affirming this interpretation, he states elsewhere that "beauty is not in the head or the heart, but in the abdomen" (Leach 1975, 123). The mind and body must be united, he asserts, which is certainly not always the case, even with highly acclaimed potters (Leach 1975, 90). As *aikidō* teaches, learning to live from the one point, from the abdomen, requires lengthy and sustained practice, over and above the practice of just martial technique. For both Yanagi and Hamada, what is required is something akin to "intuition," in the sense of seeing and acting from a place that is at least independent of, if not actually prior to, thinking. The most literal meaning of "intuition" is "direct seeing," or unmediated experiencing. D. T. Suzuki explains that "intuition" has various meanings, but that the primary meaning concerns coming directly into contact with the absolute, with reality itself. He confesses, however, that "I have come to think that 'feeling' is a better term than 'intuition,' for the experience Zen claims to have—'feeling' in its deepest, broadest, and most basic sense, and not the 'feeling' of psychologists . . . [but] the experience the human mind has when it is identified with the totality of things or when the finite becomes conscious of the infinite residing in it" (Suzuki 1959, 219fn). This becoming aware of the infinite residing in the individual artistic creation can only be experienced by one's bodymind as something akin to feeling. Those who have this capacity are often the uneducated and childlike. Such a state is encouraged by Zen training. The *kōans*, and other practices in Zen, are designed to still the active mind, to block off all avenues of resolution and mediation, leading one to experience the just-now and right-here. Yanagi praises the tea masters of the past for their ability to just see: "they saw; before all else, they saw" (Yanagi 1972, 177). He explains what he means by the fact that they "saw" by turning his attention to "seeing directly" in relation to Tea:

> Most people look through some medium, generally imposing thoughts, personal tastes, and habits between the

eye and the object. Assuredly, the result is different points of view; but it is quite another thing to see directly. Seeing directly constitutes a direct communion between the eye and the object. Unless a thing is seen without mediation, the thing itself cannot be grasped. Only the men who possess this capacity of direct perception are true masters of Tea, just as those who can see God with immediacy are the real priests worthy of the name. True men of Tea are masters of the power of seeing. (Yanagi 1972, 177)

This unmediated seeing of the old tea masters is best described, in philosophical terms, by Nishida Kitarō, who refers to it as "pure experience," a term he borrowed from the American philosopher and psychologist, William James (1842–1910), although he adapted it to the Japanese context of understanding and for his own specific purposes. Pure experience is non-dual experience, a concept not warmly embraced by most thinkers in the West. A notable exception is Robert K. C. Forman, who provides the philosophical basis for "pure consciousness" from a Western perspective (Forman 1999). But in Japan, non-dualism has a long history, most notably in Zen Buddhist and Buddhist thought. Yanagi himself, in his chapter "The Buddhist Idea of Beauty" in *The Unknown Craftsman*, argues that "true beauty" is a beauty beyond the antithesis of the beautiful and the ugly: "true beauty exists in the realm where there is no distinction between the beautiful and the ugly, a realm that is described as 'prior to beauty and ugliness' or as a state where beauty and ugliness are as yet unseparated'" (Yanagi 1972, 130). Such seeing, like pure experience itself, is seeing prior to the dualistic distinction-making of the intellect, and it intuits things as they are in their depths, in themselves, rather than comparatively. Pure experience signifies "a condition of true experience without the addition of the least thought or reflection" (Nishida 1990, 1). Nishida's gloss on this bold claim is important:

The moment of seeing a color or hearing a sound, for example, is prior not only to the thought that the color or sound is the activity of an external object or that one is sensing it, but also to the judgment of what the color or sound might be. In this regard, pure experience is identical with direct experience. When one directly experiences one's own state of consciousness, there is not yet a subject or an object, and knowing and its object are completely unified. This is the most refined type of experience. (Nishida 1990, 3–4)

Robert Forman, in agreement with this quotation which emphasizes the direct experience of one's own state of consciousness, contends that "sheer awareness" is "unalloyed with the usual intentional content," and is an instance of, and perhaps the only instance of, "knowledge-by-identity" (Forman 1999, 110–19). The focus of pure experience is always on the present, the "now." The "now" does not depend on the dualism of past or future, but is just what it is, unmediated by anything additional.

Relating Zen teaching to aesthetics, Yanagi insists that:

> the final objective of Zen Buddhists is, of course, liberation from all duality; good and evil, true and false, beautiful and ugly, one's self and others, life and death, consciousness and unconsciousness. All such dualistic forms must be discarded. Day in, day out Zen Buddhists undergo rigorous training to that end, for so long as they are trapped in the polarized world, they are unable to achieve peace of mind, to attain Buddhahood. A true artist is not one who chooses beauty in order to eliminate ugliness, he is not one who dwells in a world that distinguishes between the beautiful and the ugly, but rather he is one who has entered the realm where strife between the two cannot exist. Only in the work of a man who has attained this state of mind is there no room for encroachment by the ugly or for the kind of relative beauty that is comprehensible only as an antithesis of the ugly. (Yanagi 1972, 137)

We live and work in a dualistic world. Yet Zen teaches that we can be free of the constraints of duality, even while thriving in a dualistic world, if we can only see beyond or beneath this perspective, for "the Zen admonition against remaining in duality is actually a warning not to be enslaved by it, for even if one dwells in duality one may still be free provided one is the master who employs duality" (Yanagi 1972, 138).

Non-Dualistic Awareness

The seat of non-dualistic awareness is to be found in one's own mind. Looking into one's own nature (*kenshō*), one finds the undifferentiated, the unborn, nothingness. We are afforded a glimpse of ultimate reality prior to differentiation and form: we experience our own Buddha-nature. Since "Buddha is no other than an incarnation of Non-dualism" (Yanagi 1972, 144), then we, too, in our depths, are Buddha also. And since the root of dualism is the ego, which has separated itself off from all other things, then the transcendence of the chains of duality will require the negation of the ordinary ego-self. When the ego is put to rest, then truly great art becomes a genuine possibility. Without that spiritual transformation, art remains self-preoccupied and calculated, rather than spontaneous and trans-individual. In fact, Yanagi and Hamada both extol the artist-craftsperson who leaves his or her work unsigned. Creation is not about fame or fortune, but about a practiced sense of the appropriate and, at times, the sublime. Almost all of the really good potters were anonymous, Yanagi insists. Similarly, when Hamada was asked why he did not sign his own pots (although he did so, for a time, as a younger potter), he responded, "If you cannot see who it is by, it is either because the pot is bad, or because you are blind." He did, however, sign the boxes in which his pots were packaged, and when asked why he signed the boxes, he replied, "I cannot escape the social obligation." Bernard Leach, who recorded the conversation, added that Hamada "explained that it should not be a question of whether or not the pot is signed, but of the spirit in which it is made" (Leach 1975, 93).

Yet there remains a paradox to be dealt with: the Zen Buddhist practices long and hard to become childlike, and many artists strive for decades before finally reaching the point where their work appears to arise spontaneously from their depths. Nevertheless, what is striking about both Yanagi and Hamada is their love of ancient Chinese, Korean, and Okinawan pottery, which was made by ordinary workers who toiled long hours making the same type of pottery over and over again. These were simple, uneducated people, who likely knew nothing of Zen practice or its equivalent, or about a Buddhist theory of beauty. But what they did discover, especially the child-workers, through practice and repetition in their work, was how to be liberated from dualistic opposition, although none of them would have had any idea that this was happening to them. They were not concerned about beauty and ugliness, but, for example, they only had to move their brush quickly, unhesitatingly, if drawing designs on the pottery. Furthermore, "they forgot themselves as they worked, or perhaps it would be more correct to say that they worked in a world so free they were able to forget themselves" (Yanagi 1972, 135). They worked anonymously, settled within a tradition, that was "the accumulation of the experience and wisdom of many generations, in what Buddhists call the Given Power—an aggregate power that in all cases transcends the individual" (Yanagi 1972, 135). So it is that an individual piece is not merely the product of a gifted individual, but rather of the "Given Power of tradition" speaking loudly and effortlessly through an individual. As the result of the labor and inspiration of generations of potters, the beauty produced was not thought to be personal, so there was no need to identify its maker. Indeed, "to the craftsman, tradition is both the savior and the benefactor. When he follows it, the distinction between talented and untalented individuals all but disappears: any craftsman can unfailingly produce a beautiful work of art. But if he loses sight of the long tradition behind him, his work can only be that of a bumbling incompetent. Tradition never asks who is enlisting its help" (Yanagi 1972, 135–36). Hamada himself endorsed this spirit when he responded to a question about his largest kiln in Mashiko, a potters' village north of Tokyo. The question had to do with why he needed such a large kiln (it held more than ten thousand pots, though he also had a smaller kiln made of mud):

> If a kiln is small, I might be able to control it completely, that is to say, my own self can become a controller, a master of the kiln. But man's own self is but a small thing after all. When I work at the large kiln, the power of my own self becomes so feeble that it cannot control it adequately. It means that for the large kiln, the power that is beyond me is necessary. Without the mercy of such invisible power I cannot get good pieces. One of the reasons

why I wanted to have a large kiln is because I want to be
a potter, if I may, who works more in grace than in his
own power. You know [that] nearly all the best old pots
were done in huge kilns. (Yanagi 1972, 224)

I have visited that sprawling mud kiln, which meanders up a
small hillside, and what struck me forcibly was the utter simplicity, even humility, of it. Consisting only of dried mud and clay,
with black smoke billowing from it as more wood was placed in
its yawning fire pit, it stood in such sharp contrast to the up to
date commercial "ovens" I was used to seeing in potteries in the
West. This homespun creation seemed out of place as the source
of some of the most dramatic and dynamic firings in the world.
The smaller kiln was simply a smaller version of the same construction, and held about one-tenth as many pots. I was similarly
struck by his studio, which was more like a simple farm building,
a chicken-coop-shaped structure with a dirt floor, a woodstove
with an aluminum tea kettle on top, and three potter's wheels.
As a Living National Treasure, Hamada could have built his
dream studio, and his dream kiln. In fact, he did. It was the simple, unpretentious workshop studio and kiln complex that I have
just described. What he wanted to create were pots as simple and
healthy and clean as those which had been created by simple folk
in China and Korea and Okinawa. For him, these pots represented the "state of the art," and not the ones made by those
who were trying so hard to do so by having the "right" tools, the
"right" location, and the "right" showplace for their wares. As I
settled into his studio and we talked about pottery and the Zen
spirit, I was overwhelmed by the sheer comfort of the place. I felt
at home, as though I had been allowed to visit a great man in his
comfortable clothes and slippers, rather than in his finest and
showiest attire. Nothing about the studio, the kiln, or the man
was done to impress. He was utterly approachable, utterly humble and sincere in his work and in his talk, seemingly unaware
that visitors outside of his compound would fall to the ground in
his honor, forehead to the earth in recognition of his greatness,
whenever they caught sight of him. Oblivious to the reactions
around him, he was concerned only with beauty, and it was on a
tour of beauty that he took me that day at his farm retreat.

Hamada: Teacher and Collector

Hamada lectured and taught the world over, demonstrating his abilities and insights. He spent much of his extra time on such tours browsing through antique shops, second-hand shops, art shops, looking for examples of craft objects of unusual worth. He regretted the fact that they were often simply sold off, or disappeared into the homes of the rich, never to emerge again, or were simply lost as unimportant. As the curator of the Folk-Craft Museum in Tokyo, he asked the Japanese government to allow him to purchase choice examples of fine craft that he encountered. They agreed enthusiastically, and he set off with an open budget to bring back the greatest examples of folk-craft that he could find. The objects discovered and purchased were either on display at the museum or kept in one of the several storehouses on his compound. These old-style buildings were high-roofed, with balconies for additional storage, and with the traditional sunken fire pits in the center that sent their smoke out through a hole in the ceiling high above. The smoke hole was covered by a small roof on stilts, but still open all around to let the smoke escape.

What was quite remarkable was the tour of beauty he took me on that afternoon, after his morning work at the wheel was complete. We looked at trunks from Spain, dressers from Europe and North America, armoires from Quebec, huge clay pots from Okinawa, tables from Germany, jade pieces from several places in the Far East, and pocket watches from England. I have never seen so much beauty in one place, and, as he pulled out his favorites, he would sit down on the floor, across from me, carefully unwrap a piece, and then explain why it was the incredible instance of its kind that it was. We would talk about each piece, touch each piece in order to get the feel of it, and then he would slowly and carefully rewrap it, for this, too, was part of the journey of appreciation that he had taken me on. Rewrapping is a chore, to be left behind for someone else to take care of, only if it is allowed to be. For Hamada, the rewrapping, the care of each piece, was part of being drenched in the beauty of each object. It was done as a sign of respect and appreciation. I had been dropped into an ideal, almost imaginary, world whose focus was on the creating and appreciating of beauty. Beauty was the driving focus of the place, and the driving force of the man. I was overwhelmed by what it was that he had shown me by example: how to live in the "now" of each and every exquisite piece. We shared the objects and the space together in this once in a lifetime encounter.

Hamada's sense of working in grace and flowing with an invisible power that is beyond his finite power, calculations, and intentions, echoes Yanagi's focus on *tariki* (other-power). Earlier in this study, in the chapter on the Way of Tea, Dennis Hirota was identified as a scholar of Tea who emphasized the particular importance of Pure Land teaching on the Japanese Arts. Zen's emphasis is on *jiriki* (self-power), but what Yanagi, Hamada, and Hirota seem to agree on is the additional importance of other-power in Japanese thought and on the Japanese arts. What seems to resonate with all of them is the sense that one becomes a vehicle through which the divine acts in this world. The "heart behind the hands" is not just one's own heart but the greater heart of tradition, and Buddha, or God, or the cosmos speaking and acting through us. Regarding *tariki* and the making of humble multipurpose bowls in Korea, now priceless because of their simple beauty as tea bowls, these authentic creations stand in sharp contrast to the deliberate attempts to willfully imitate the naive simplicity and beauty in Japanese *raku* tea bowls. The emphasis is on willful intent, rather than on the spontaneous unfolding of a style that has no intent or pretense. Yanagi writes:

Perhaps the best way of explaining this is by a comparison of the early and later implements of Tea. The former came from either China, or more particularly, Korea. They had an enormous influence upon Japanese taste and Japanese craftsmen began to imitate them, mainly under the patronage of the later masters. . . . A comparison between the Korean Ido bowls and the Japanese Raku Tea-bowls is sufficient to make this quite clear. The Raku bowls were made with deliberate effort, the Korean bowls were effortless products of daily living and were not even intended for Tea. In theory the Japanese bowls might have been expected to be better, but in actuality the Korean are far better. The reason for this is clear if one considers which follows more faithfully the Zen warning to "avoid the artificial." (Yanagi 1972, 125)

Yanagi adds that trying to reproduce the Korean style is an instance of *jiriki*, whereas what is needed is *tariki* (the abandonment of attempts at self-reliance, and relying on grace instead). The imperfect, utterly simple, and natural creations of nameless craftsmen were not the result of studied technique but, rather, flowed forth through their hands and brushes, yielding unforgettable and still-treasured results. It was the tea men who first saw this *wabi-sabi* beauty and then codified it as the impeccable sense of the truly beautiful: a beauty which is beyond perfection, symmetry, and flawlessness. Hamada grasped this so well when he mused that we cannot truly complete anything in our lives:

> After all, when everything is arranged and complete there is nothing more to be said. . . . If one says "finished," there is no life there anymore, but if one says "unfinished," life continues, movement goes on. I was going to write a piece [in which I say that] . . . my work is always unfinished, [but] I still have not written it. That is, after all, the meaning of unfinished. When something is unfinished, it is finished. (Leach 1975, 89)

The conclusion reached is profound: "when something is unfinished, it is finished." This phrase encapsulates the Japanese sense of beauty, what it is that the tea men saw, what the simple Chinese, Korean, and Okinawan peasant-craftsmen and craftswomen achieved in the midst of their weary work, and what it was that Hamada exhibited in almost everything he wrought: *shibui. Shibui* is the verb, *shibusa* the noun, and the only way to convey the complexity of the simplicity which is *shibui*, is through a cluster of words. Yanagi suggests "austere," "subdued," "restrained," "quietness," "depth," "simplicity," "purity," "unobtrusive." He writes that "the word '*shibusa*' is in everyday use in Japan, and the criterion it sets up is taken as a measure to determine the depth or shallowness of the beauty of any given object" (Yanagi 1972, 149).

The most treasured tea bowls were unsigned bowls made for everyday use: "the early tea masters chose not a single piece that was made in order to be appreciated." Instead, they chose bowls that were made to be used. Hamada, too, stressed that he was "not interested in making or creating something novel or refined or acceptable from the standpoint of the usual idea of beauty, but that [he] . . . was aiming at making correct and healthy things, pottery that is practical and not forced, that responds to the nature of the materials. . . . [he] did not want to make something outwardly beautiful, but to begin from the inside; health and correctness were more important" (Hamada 1975, 79).

. . . and Ethics?

Little has been said about ethics directly, and certainly nothing about ethical theory. On the other hand, nearly everything said about pottery and beauty is instructional as to how to live one's life with integrity and honesty. The selfless living of a life of simplicity, refined (not cultured) taste, the realization of the open-endedness of a life lived in the midst of the ever-changing flux of existence, and the necessity of being-here-right-now, all have ethical implications. The selfless awareness of "pure experience" is necessary if one is to encounter another as a thou. Whether human or rock, textured moss or clay pot, a responsiveness is required that is impossible if one's ego-self is the center of focus. Like the Zen landscape designer Masuno Shunmyo in chapter 3, Hamada listened to his materials. He decided how to glaze and/or decorate a pot by intuition, which is unimpeded receptivity: "I simply look at the pot and ask it what it wants" (Leach 1975, 134). Whatever answer was needed emerged from his "lower abdomen," the same *hara* or one point of *aikidō* that attaches us to the universal, to the divine, to a tradition which is greater than any individual, and to the grace of Amida Buddha, or God, or Allah, or Yahweh, or to the energy of the *kami*. And like all other human activities, Japanese ethics must arise, ultimately, from the same source as well.

Nishida maintained that value judgments arise from "the internal demands of consciousness, not from without," from an "internal necessity" which leads us to recognize the good and to do it (Nishida 1990, 122–23). In comparing goodness and beauty, Nishida writes that the concept of good approaches, or is remarkably similar to, that of beauty:

Beauty is felt when things are realized like ideals are realized, which means for things to display their original nature. Just as flowers are most beautiful when they

manifest their original nature, humans attain the pinnacle of beauty when they express their original nature. In
this regard the good is beauty. No matter how valueless
conduct might appear when seen in light of the great demands of human nature, when it is truly natural conduct
emerging from the innate talents of the person, it evokes
a sense of beauty. In the moral realm this conduct likewise gives rise to a kind of magnanimous feeling. . . .
The good, conceived of as the development and comple-
tion of the self, amounts to our obeying the laws of the
reality called the self. That is, to unite with the true reality of the self is the highest good. The laws of morality
thus come to be included in the laws of reality, and we
are able to explain the good in terms of the true nature
of the reality called the self. (Nishida 1990, 125–26)

The "good is the realization of personality," which coincides
with a human being's deepest natural inclinations. Ethics is not
something strapped onto a personality, but arises out of the
depths of a personality, but only in Dōgen's sense of the self beyond the ego-self: "To study the way is to study the self. To
study the self is to forget the self. To forget the self is to be actualized by myriad things. When actualized by myriad things, your
body and mind as well as the bodies and minds of others drop
away" (Dōgen 1985, 70). Ethics is not an external set of rules
and regulations, but a spontaneous expression of who it is that
one has become. Once the self is out of the way, our greatest
goals are now internalized such that aims and inclinations "unite
automatically." What you are, and what you ought to do, are
one and the same. The result is a giving rise "to love for our fellow humans and [we] come to accord with the supremely good
goal—good conduct that is perfect and true." Thus, "morality is
not a matter of seeking something apart from the self—it is simply the discovery of something within the self. . . . No matter
how small the enterprise, a person who constantly works out of
love for his or her fellow humans realizes the great personality of
all humankind" (Nishida 1990, 144–45). That is to say, one who
has come to realize the authentic urges of one's deepest levels of
heretofore unconscious awareness has discovered truths which

are the same at the depths of each and every other person. The greatest spiritual leaders have come to similar conclusions about ethical requirements precisely because those conclusion arose out of the depths of human nature which, while unknown to most, are common to all. Perhaps we might refer to this as the "great tradition of morality," for it is simply to recollect what untold others have discovered and rediscovered time and again.

Plato, in his *Protagoras*, playfully engages in literary criticism, recalling a dispute between a poet and a statesman over the proper interpretation of a poem. The issue concerns whether it is hard to become good, or hard to be good. Playful as the discussion is, Plato's Socrates resolves the issue by using a passage from Hesiod as the solution, and also as a statement of his own position:

> On the one hand, 'tis difficult for a man to become good,
> For the gods have made virtue the reward of toil;
> But on the other hand, when you have climbed the height,
> Then, to retain virtue, however difficult the acquisition, is
>   easy. (Plato 1956, 340d)

The arduous task, both for Plato and the Japanese, is the practice of the self-cultivation needed to reach inner goodness. For Plato, it was symbolized by the long journey out of the cave, beginning with the breaking of the chains of ordinary seeing, and culminating with the slow adjustment of the eyes to the brilliance of the truth itself. It required several decades of dedicated study and practice to become a philosopher. Within the Japanese tradition, the exception to this is the appeal to other-power, which makes it possible even for the most humble to be reborn, more or less on the spot. What follows from this, however, is a lifetime of renewal and dedication. But whether self-power or other-power is engaged, the realm one enters at the culmination of one's quest is that of non-dualistic affinity. It is at that point that all others become thous, become beloved, and one's relationship with the world, both human and nonhuman, is now one of love.

Nishida sums this up best in his magnificent essay "Knowledge and Love." He begins by affirming that love and knowledge are fundamentally the same activities. It is the activity of the union of subject and object, of uniting with things. To come to

know another requires the elimination of our own prejudices, aspirations, and agendas: "To love something is to cast away the
self and unite with that other. When self and other join with no
gap between them, true feelings of love first arise. To love a
flower is to unite with the flower, and to love the moon is to
unite with the moon" (Nishida 1990, 174). He then applies this
sense of selfless unity to our relationships with people:

> The love between a parent and child comes forth only
> when the parent becomes the child and the child becomes
> the parent. Because the parent becomes the child, the
> parent feels each of the child's gains or losses as his or
> her own; and because the child becomes the parent, the
> child feels as his or her own each instance of joy or sad-
> ness on the part of the parent. The more we discard the
> self and become purely objective or selfless, the greater
> and deeper our love becomes. We advance from the love
> between parent and child or husband and wife to the
> love between friends, and from there to the love of hu-
> mankind. The Buddha's love extended even to birds,
> beasts, grasses, and trees. (Nishida 1990, 174)

In order to know a thing, we must first love it, and this necessi-
tates becoming totally absorbed in that which is to be known, to
be loved: "We forget the self, and at this point an incomprehensible power beyond the self functions alone in all of its majesty;
there is neither subject nor object, but only the true union of subject and object" (Nishida 1990, 174–75). When there is no distinction between self and other, it is then possible to feel what
the other is feeling, or, as Nishida phrases it, it is possible to
intuit the other's feelings: "love is the power by which we grasp
ultimate reality. Love is the deepest knowledge of things. Analytical, inferential knowledge is a superficial knowledge, and it cannot grasp reality. We can reach reality only through love. Love is
the culmination of knowledge" (Nishida 1990, 175).

Nishida concludes his essay on knowledge and love by ad-
dressing the relationship between self-power and other-power:

> Subjectivity is self-power and objectivity is other-power.
> To know and love a thing is to discard self-power and

embody the faithful heart that believes in other-power. If we assume that the work of one's life is not separate from knowledge and love, then day in and day out we are functioning upon faith in other-power. Both learning and morality are the glory of Buddha, and religion is the culmination of knowledge in love. In distinct individual phenomena, learning and morality are bathed in the glorious light of other-power. . . . Both views [self-power and other-power] have their own distinctive features, but they are identical in essence. (Nishida 1990, 176)

Summary

Throughout this study, I hope it has become apparent that each of the artistic traditions investigated displays the characteristic of selfless love of their focal objects. For *aikidō*, it was love of the universal, and an unwavering focus on *ki* energy. The goal was the transformation of the self in order to make love the standard of action with other people and other things. In landscape gardening, it was necessary to become one with the materials and the site, to listen to what they had to say, to create a loving space and interconnected network of stones, plants, and earth. The Way of Tea insisted on the tea master becoming one with his or her guests, and one with the delicate sounds, smells, tastes, and sights of the tea room and the outer garden. The aim was to create an environment of loving togetherness, of selfless interaction, and of timeless awareness of the greater reality which manifests here and now during each and every moment. This is the moment and the place to love, for there will never be another exactly like it. Do not let it slip by, unnoticed and unappreciated. The Way of Flower Arranging begins with the love of flowers, and the student proceeds by selflessly intuiting what is the natural "bent" of the flowers and branches, and then, from a place of unity, extending all the way to enlightenment, the flowers and branches are assembled in such a way as to bring out the best in the plants, not just the best in the arranger. Such acts need to be selfless, coupled with a spontaneous recognition of what the plants themselves want. So, a loving relationship must be established which can be discerned in the quality of a flower arrangement. And the potter listens to the pot, as Hamada did, working in the grace of a power which goes far beyond the intellect and experience of the potter.

We seem to live and work in the grace of a power which sustains us all, Hamada believed, and yet it is we who work. Self-power and other-power unite in the person of the artist, and particularly of the moral artist. The greatest artistic achievements, and the greatest acts of moral kindness, both emerge out of an inner space, an emptiness, which responds to the other in such a way as to bring out the best in it, and therefore in oneself as well. Greatness of character, whether artistic or moral, arises out of an emptiness, a nothingness, which allows contact that is drenched with an empathetic capacity to identify with the highs and lows of another, that can comprehend the deepest wants and needs of another, and can reach out in love so as to bring the other to a higher place than before. A true friend and lover raises the beloved to a higher level of awareness and functioning, helps to make the other better than before there was love directed his or her way. It is a love that does not seek to control but only to work within the limits that the other requires. This is the true meaning of "respect," for it does not mean that one does for the other what one would want done for oneself, but rather that one does for the other what the other, in his or her deepest levels of being, would want done to and for him or her self. To love another is to care, to nurture, and to protect that other. Milton Mayeroff, in his remarkable book *On Caring*, concludes by observing that "through caring and being cared for man experiences himself as part of nature; we are closest to a person or an idea when we help it grow." He then goes on to say:

> There is a rock-bottom quality about living the meaning of my life that goes, oddly enough, with greater awareness of life's inexhaustible depths; it is as if life is ordinary and "nothing special" when it is most extraordinary. And although we find a deep-seated intelligibility in life, the last word is with the unfathomable character of existence which, like a pedal point in a piece of music, pervades and colors life. (Mayeroff 1971, 87)

This book has been about that deeper place, both within the individual and the grand cosmos itself, which, while never directly seen, is the lining which shapes and sustains everything that is. It is this lining, this background or profound depth, that each of the arts presented here has attempted to provide intimations of and, to the degree that they succeed, they have provided magnificent examples of loving relationships along the way. Relationships of love are not limited to human ones: every "it" is also a "thou," although it takes a master to recognize this simple, yet profound, truth.

Conclusion

I have nothing against sports, they train the body and develop stamina and endurance. But the spirit of competition
and power that presides over them is not good, it reflects a
distorted vision of life. The root of the martial arts is not
there. . . . In the spirit of Zen and Budō everyday life becomes
the contest. There must be awareness at every moment—
getting up in the morning, working, eating, going to bed.
That is the place for the mastery of self.
　　　　　—Deshimaru, *The Zen Way to the Martial Arts*

One cannot help but be impressed by the cultural and spiritual
depth of the arts in Japan, and by the number of people who still
practice those arts today, if only intermittently, incorporating
them into their lives even in this age of computers and mass
media. That the popularity of the arts has clearly diminished
cannot be denied, and yet there is something of a rediscovery occurring in the schools, which are increasingly incorporating the
arts and their practice into the curriculum. Yet the point and
force of deep traditions in any culture is not simply their popularity, but the effect they have on ways of thinking, feeling, and
living. This influence can be seen in the ordinary Japanese citi-
zen in many ways, such as in their love of nature, through their
attendance at natural seasonal highlights including the blossom-
ing of the many cherry trees in spring, the bright red of Japanese
maples in the autumn, and the haunting beauty of iris beds and
hanging wisteria. Furthermore, one finds a "Japanese room"
even in most modern, western-style homes, which includes

tatami mats and a *tokonoma* for displaying pottery, flowers, and a hanging scroll (all reminiscent of the tea room). Moreover, deep traditions also serve as repositories of wisdom of a kind that may well help all of us to survive and flourish in a future which seems increasingly dangerous, self-destructive, and ecologically perilous. The wisdom of Japanese culture is not to be found in mimicking the past, but in adapting the past to modern circumstances. It includes a focus on the whole rather than on the part: a vision of eternity and not just a concentration on the present and the immediate future. At the same time, it extols the importance of the moment, the now, but against the background of eternity. In this sense, one is taught to live in the midst of self-contradictory identity, as Nishida would phrase it, by being in the now, and yet, being aware of eternity as it "lines" and enriches each and every now we experience. Just as we live by dying (each day is a day closer to death) and die by living (we die by living each and every day, hopefully with zest and delight), so eternity is manifest in, and only in, the now of individual things, meaning that each now and all individuals are self-manifestations of the whole of eternity.

Ethics and Self-Transformation

What makes Japanese ethics so difficult to grasp concretely is that so much of what counts as ethics in Japan is attitudinal. In *Encounter with Enlightenment*, I try to outline the attitudinal changes which Shintō facilitates. Let me here mention a few of these attitudes which can be taken as constitutive of the essence of "Japaneseness": they include, *michi*, sound character, integrity; *harai*, genuine purity of body, mind, and heart; *makoto*, sincerity, i.e., honesty, truthfulness, trustworthiness, and a genuine desire to strive for self-perfection, or, as I prefer, self-development; *wa*, which includes both group or social harmony and harmony within the family and within each individual; *akarusa*, cheerfulness of heart, which manifests as a lack of moodiness on display, in public; *kansha*, a spirit of thankfulness; and *kenshin*, a total offering of what one is, not out of a sense of duty, but as a matter of the heart. In *Encounter with Enlightenment*, I describe this as being:

akin to the devotion of *agape* in Greek thought, which is deeper and purer than ordinary love, and it is unconditional. It is perfectly spontaneous, arising from the heart for no extrinsic or calculated reasons. . . . Between human beings, the appropriate relationship is that of benevolence (*itsu-kushi-mi*). This implies *uyamau*, or showing proper respect, courtesy, displaying the correct etiquette. (Carter 2001, 48)

The attitudes are many, and also include as you may recall from what has gone before, tranquility as a sense of peacefulness, a love of the simple, the rustic, the aged which is perceived as being robust in spirit notwithstanding its years, and so on. It does seem that the Japanese emphasis in ethics is on attitudinal teaching and transformation, rather than on rules and regulations, or theoretical justification for what already counts as maturity in Japanese culture. For the unthinking, or for those not well brought up, or for those with psychosocial illnesses, immersion in subtle environments which aim to teach the right values may well be insufficient. Reason and law must establish standards, for society and its institutions must have rules in order to operate with efficiency and safety. Yet the primary teaching in Japanese society is done through the rituals of Shintō, Buddhism, and Confucianism, and through the day-to-day practice of the arts. The arts as practiced promote the ideals of sociality, of Japaneseness, and of individual health. Given the many books and articles written on and about Japan, most of us are familiar with the successes of Japan as a culture. There are, of course, failures as well, like Pearl Harbor, the brutal wartime treatment of the Chinese and Koreans, the unwillingness of Japan to refrain from whaling in spite of the pleas from other countries that are trying to enforce a whaling ban in an attempt to ward off the threat of extinction, or Japan's inherent sexism. Like any culture, Japan does not always, or even often enough, live up to its own ideals. Nevertheless, when one compares it to other modern cultural traditions, it has an abundance of unexpected positive qualities which are tangible to anyone who spends even a little time in Japan. Still, it is worth noting that serious critical studies have been written detailing less positive aspects of Japanese culture, ranging from a decided lack of social ethics in Buddhism and Zen, to an exaggerated sense of Japan's "specialness," to the evident support given by Zen Buddhist teachers for Japan's involvement and actions in the Second World War.[1]

Keeping these criticisms in mind, and not wanting to idolize Japan, but at the same time wishing to point out its many strengths, I think it must be admitted that Japan is comparatively exemplary in terms of the quality of life that prevails and the sensitivity to others that can be discerned. It may well be true in some instances that this caring for others is less heartfelt and more an uneasiness about being seen not to care, yet it remains true, nonetheless, that it is still a culture that encourages a remarkable degree of other-directedness and caring, that includes a respectfulness extending from one's ancestors to one's neighbors. T. R. Reid has compared Japan to several major western countries in order to emphasize the relative peacefulness and harmony which one finds in Japan:

> in statistical terms . . . serious crimes are rare events compared with what happens in the rest of the world. There are about 7.5 murders each year for every 100,000 Americans. England's murder rate is roughly 5.5 murders per 100,000 people. Germany has 4.3 per 100,000,

---

1. The best single source for an in-depth discussion of the involvement of Japanese intellectuals in the Second World War, and an exaggerated sense of nationalism, is *Rude Awakenings: Zen, the Kyoto School and the Question of Nationalism*, James W. Heisig and John C. Maraldo, eds. (Honolulu: University of Hawaii Press, 1994). A hard-hitting and extremely critical study of Zen Buddhism and its support for Japan's involvement in the Second World War is Brian (Daizen) A. Victoria's *Zen at War* (New York: Weatherhill, Inc., 1997). Peter N. Dale's *The Myth of Japanese Uniqueness* further examines Japan's frequent emphasis on its "special" status among the people of the Far East. Christopher Ives, in *Zen Awakening and Society*, critically evaluates the lack of a social ethics in Zen (Honolulu: University of Hawaii Press, 1992). An account of ethics and Zen and Zen's relationship to the Second World War can be found in my *Encounter with Enlightenment: A Study of Japanese Ethics* (Albany: State University of New York Press, 2001), chapter 5. Ives's essay in *Rude Awakenings* questions whether enlightenment is a guarantee that one will act ethically (in Buddhist terms, acting with wisdom and compassion), and Bernard Faure questions the entire apparatus for determining whether one has or has not attained enlightenment and the states of "master" (*Chan Insights and Oversights* [Princeton: Princeton University Press, 1993].)

France has 4.1. In Japan, the murder rate is below 1.0
per 100,000. . . . The most striking difference is in the
rates of property crimes—arson, burglary, robbery, car
theft, etc. According to the American criminologist
David Bailey, the United States has about 140 times as
many robberies per year as Japan does. In Tokyo, there
are about 500 robberies per year—a little more than one
per day. New York City has about 215 reported robberies every day. The reason people don't use car alarms
in Japan—even though most cars are left out on the
street at night—is that auto theft is not a problem there.
(Reid 1999, 23–24)

Added to these remarkable statistics regarding crime rates are the
countless ways in which the visitor is impressed by the politeness,
the considerateness, and the generosity of the Japanese, notwithstanding individual instances to the contrary.

The Train to Takayama

I could cite many examples of this human-heartedness during my
nine journeys to Japan, the longest of which was a two-year visit,
but one stands out as a testament to Japanese other-directedness,
as well as to their love of nature. It is an encounter which I have
previously described in *Becoming Bamboo* (Carter 1992,
30–33). I had found my way to Nagoya, from Kyoto, and was
setting out on the train to Hida Takayama (in Gifu Prefecture),
often called "little Kyoto," and reputed to be one of the most traditional and beautiful villages in all Japan. The town itself is a
living museum, featuring houses that have been preserved in almost the exact condition that they were in three hundred years
ago. The district called San-machi Suji was the traditional home
of the Takayama merchants and sake brewers, including inns,
shops, and taverns. The train that would take me there was akin
to the silver Budd Liners of North America: two motorized pas-
senger cars, crammed with Japanese heading to the mountains
and the other scenic splendors of the area. Only a handful of
empty seats remained. I was the only foreigner—*gaijin*—on
board, and was left with a double seat all to myself.

The train began to make its way when, suddenly, there was commotion in every direction in the car, and as I glanced around, it was evident that all eyes were on me. The stares were good-natured, as the slight smiles and mischievous eyes made evident. Everyone else knew that the train was about to reverse its direction, taking the other leg of the "y" turnabout, and every seat had to be spun around to face in the opposite direction. It sounded like a machine shop in full production, and I got to my feet and searched for the release mechanism. I could not locate it anywhere and, at six feet four inches tall, I was desperately trying to avoid hitting my head on the low ceiling overhead. I glanced around to see if others were still completing their change, a technique that I would come to use often in Japan to enable me to appear experienced when trying to behave more or less as the Japanese do. Do I eat the leaf that the beans are cooked on, however aesthetically beautiful it might be, or do I simply scrape the beans off and leave the crispy leaf as mere garnish? This time my glance around the car netted me no last-minute instruction as to how the Japanese had unlocked their chairs. Instead, it revealed that every pair of eyes on board now showed intense merriment. It was a delicious moment when my confusion at why we were doing all this was met by their recognition of my inability to decipher either the need or the remedy.

In the briefest of instants, thirty passengers came rushing toward me to help unlatch and then turn my seat. They did so with much good humor and evident friendliness. Everyone wanted to help, to break the tension that had afforded a moment of shared delight, and when I laughed back to indicate that I shared in the humor of the awkward situation, a bond of some sort was created. The ice had melted and, in a limited way, I was now a friend.

The train stopped, then began retracing its steps, and at a switch veered sharply to the right. Having reversed our direction, we were now on our way to Takayama, and rather than facing backward, with all of us now facing forward. Next occurred an unexpected series of events. A few minutes along our journey we passed by the usual rice paddies and charming farmhouses. In near unison the passengers intoned an appreciative "aaahhh-hhh," and two Japanese rushed to my side to explain in halting English that the cloth fish-kites on the flagpoles of each farm home indicated the number of boys in the family, and sometimes the number of girls as well. Boy's Day, a holiday taken very seriously in Japan, was but a few calendar days away. On the particular flagpole that was being pointed out to me, eight kites were flying. It was evidently fertile soil, and my hosts were keen that I should share in the remarkable fact of a modern family with eight boys, and who knows how many girls, for as in many places in the world, boy children were celebrated with more heartfelt pomp than were girl children.

The train continued to speed along and, again without warning, everyone was up out of their seats and peering out of the windows opposite me. Someone tugged at my sleeve and I was whisked to the closest window opposite. My unknown guide pointed a finger as we passed by the most beautiful rapids and waterfall, which had carved a small but impressive gorge. Again the chorus of "aaahhhhhs," except this time I joined in. This rushing from side to side of the coach continued over several hours, all the way to Takayama. Together we appreciated the natural beauty of rock formations, old forests, rivers and streams, and even individual trees gnarled with age, with the weakest branches propped up by wooden crutches. Several seasoned travelers along this route were able to give enough advance warning that a "natural treasure" was soon to be in view to allow all of us to rush to the correct side, express our emotions, glance at one another with appreciative shared delight in our eyes, only to await the next treasure along the way. It was an incredible journey, both naturally, and socially.

Given my limited Japanese, it may well be asked how I was able to learn all this when I could recognize but a few words, and was able to speak even fewer. One of Japan's greatest surprises and delights is that people are more often than not willing to take the time to try to communicate with others, and succeed in doing so by means of a series of gestures, pantomimes verging on charades, and the occasional recognizable word or phrase, in your language or theirs. This communication by gesture is, of course, quite universal, but it was the gentle and fun-filled way in which it was conducted by the Japanese that touched me to the core. It was to continue later on that day when I arrived at a Japanese inn where absolutely no English was spoken. My maid-hostess sat me down on the tatami mats opposite her, in my room, and giggled at the Japanese-English dictionary I held in my hands. She reached out, gently pushed my hands and book closed with her hands, and continued holding my hands in hers for a few seconds, thereby reassuring me that somehow we would learn to speak with each other without the need of a dictionary. She then withdrew her hands, and we laughed heartily at this remarkable situation in which we found ourselves. How funny it was that we were together, and that she would have to determine my needs while I was in her care. A bath? At what time? Dinner? What time? Was I able to eat Japanese food? What did I like? Would I be reading tonight? If so, she would fold out my futon and make certain that my lamp was on the floor, by my head. The same routine was repeated for breakfast the next morning. The entire transaction still sticks in my mind as one of the true human treasures of my now several visits to Japan. We laughed at our situation, struggled with the language, gestured, laughed again, then tried once more. Rather than being an ordeal, it became a great event and has remained a vital memory for me and, I suspect, for her. She insisted that we stand side-by-side, in order to compare our relative heights, and then gauged the enormous difference in our foot size, as she slid her slippered foot next to mine, looking up, and giggling shyly as she coquettishly showed delight and surprise at the difference. We had created a language of our own and, like kids eating candy-cordials and licking their lips with pleasure, we were enjoying every moment of this no longer out of place encounter in verbal silence.

The next morning I was up at the break of dawn. A light rain was falling, and I decided to take a walk before breakfast. As I exited the small inn where I was staying, I saw just ahead the oldest portion of Takayama. Dark, aged, and weather-worn timber-sided buildings, usually one or occasionally two stories in height, lined the street. There were no neon signs, only carved wooden ones, or an artifact displayed above a doorway to indicate what kind of shop it was. A sake barrel indicating a sake shop; a broom above a straw-goods shop. There was no noise and no one else on the street except a Japanese man in his indigo blue *kimono* and wooden *geta* shoes, out for his morning walk as well. It was the Japan I had imagined, the one that I still picture, along with the gardens and temples of Kyoto. I felt myself at one with this community, this place where one could dwell without separating oneself from the natural environment, without doing it immense harm but, rather, blending in with the surroundings and cherishing both where one was and what one had built. I felt both alone and yet inextricably joined to the solitary walker ahead, as well as with the still sleeping members of the Takayama community. It was another self-contradiction that resolved itself through the very act of living, and by being in this place, at this time, while experiencing the joy of "total exertion." For a moment, this was my entire world.

This travel story is not an isolated example of the warmth and interrelational sensitivity of the Japanese. By contrast, negative examples, at least in my experience, are few and far between. Of course, there are selfish, angry, bureaucratically minded, and dour Japanese. Nevertheless, the streets and alleys are safe for both men and women, store clerks are predictably polite and upbeat, and the police are, for the most part, viewed as members of the community in which their *kōban* (police box) is situated. There are some reports of behavior breakdown in the schools, and the fast pace of life has made the Japanese more self-concerned and less other-oriented. But, at the same time, one needs only to open a map to find several Japanese moving quickly forward to offer assistance. Respect and helpfulness are culturally transmitted from the earliest years on up, and the arts are major purveyors of these attitudinal values.

Attitudes Revisited

If the Japanese approach to ethics is to develop the desired attitudes with which to face and greet life, then the practice of the various arts is central to the learning of these attitudes. Moreover, if interpersonal relationships are centrally important to the Japanese, then developing attitudes which smooth these relationships, which enhance rather than detract from them, is vital. Confucius thought of the rules of etiquette as the oil which reduced interpersonal friction, and in Japan an indirect pedagogy has developed which not only teaches what this oil consists of but how it can and should be practiced in the learning of it. The arts combine theory and practice in the same lessons. Furthermore, once the socially congenial and productive attitudes are in place, through practice as well as in theory, then the range of application can more easily be expanded beyond the family, beyond the community, even beyond the nation, to include the world and indeed the cosmos. The idea of an expanded consciousness is identified powerfully by Nishida himself. He writes:

> The development of social consciousness is not limited to the small group or the family. Our mental and physical life can develop in all of the various social groups. At the next level beyond the family, the nation unified the entirety of our conscious activity and expresses a single personality. . . . At present, the nation is the greatest expression of unified communal consciousness. But the expression of our personality cannot stop there—it demands something greater: a social union that includes all humankind. . . . If we retract the development of humankind from the beginning of history, we see that the nation is not the final goal of humankind. . . . Genuine universalism, however, does not require that each nation ceases to be. Rather, it means that each nation becomes increasingly stable, displays its distinctive characteristics, and contributes to the history of the world. (Nishida 1990, 140–41)

Just as strong and independent individuals can become friends and lovers by uniting with the "other," so nations can remain distinctively themselves while uniting with other distinctively different yet like-minded nations and cultures. It is an ideal whose time has not yet come, of course, but it is an ideal of considerable depth which may come to serve as a beacon, directing our children to develop attitudes which foster rather than inhibit the development of a diverse world, working in increasingly harmonious ways to establish a better one. Nishida finds this drive for unity not only in us, but in the very nature of the universe itself. This awareness, too, is part of his vision of an expanded consciousness: "if we assume that reality is spirit and that our spirit is simply a small part of it, then there is no reason to feel wonder at breaking beyond one's own small consciousness and realizing one great spirit. Perhaps it is our attachment to the sphere of our small consciousness that is most in error.

Great people have spiritual experiences far deeper than those of average people" (Nishida 1990, 166).

Great artists create forms that are far deeper than those of average people, as well. Ueshiba-sensei's *aikidō* presents a cosmic perspective culminating in our relationship with the universal. Landscape gardens, celebrating tea together, cut flowers floating in the nothingness of eternity, and pottery which somehow emerges from the grace of the beyond are all forms which quietly speak of the background, the lining, which constitutes their depth. One who is open to this quiet background will find that the silence becomes a whisper, and then a full-fledged roar. Those who "listen" to the arts of Japan can be whisked away on a cosmic journey without end, while remaining firmly embedded in the particular art object or form right here, right now. To listen to the roar of eternity in the present now of living is not to be other worldly but to live in the mud of reality with a joy, a newness, and a desire to care for and protect all that one sees, hears, touches, tastes, and smells. A cosmic perspective of this proportion renders even the mud underneath one's feet an encounter with the ultimate source of all things. If the mud is clay, then just imagine what it might become in the hands of a Hamada, single-mindedly extending the act of creative expression in our midst. True creation is an ongoing activity, both as the sustaining power that keeps each of us alive and as the thirst for continued self-cultivation in a cosmos of infinite expansiveness. Infinite expansion is not just a trait of the cosmos but also of the potential to be discovered within each of us. This cosmic perspective is robustly optimistic, and this is vitally important now, at a time when humanity is desperately in need of optimism. The Japanese arts are an expression of this cosmic viewpoint, and while not the only voices of healing optimism, they are voices that need to be heard. Perhaps in the few silent spaces of modern living, these voices will continue to be heard, if only as gentle whispers, barely audible above the patter of the falling rain.

GLOSSARY

agatsu. victory over oneself.

aikibujutsu. Ueshiba-sensei's first label for the new martial art that he developed, which became *aikidō*.

aikidōka. a student of *aikidō*: anyone who practices *aikidō*.

akarusa. cheerfulness of heart (*kokoro no akarusa kaikatsusa*).

bōjutsu. the art of the six-foot-long staff (*bō*).

budō. *bu* refers to the military; *budō* is the martial way: the martial arts.

bushidō. the Way of the Warrior (the *samurai*), or the warrior code.

chadō. the Way of Tea (a term used less often than the preferred *sadō* [see entry further on]).

chanoyu. the Tea ceremony (see also *chadō, sadō*).

dao. Chinese: the way, or path; previously *tao*.

dharma. Sanskrit: the teachings of the Buddha, truth, doctrine, virtue, righteousness.

dō. the Japanese equivalent of *dao*: the way, or path.

dōjō. a training hall for the practice of the martial arts; literally, "the place where we study the 'way' (*dō*)."

fudochi shinmyo ryoku. Zen master Takuan's (1573–1645) notion of "immovable wisdom" (*fudochi*), an imperceptible moving that allows one to be open to any eventuality, as communicated in a letter written by Takuan to Yagyū Munenori, founder of the Yagyū *Shinkage* tradition of swordsmanship, who served several *shōguns* at the beginning of the Edo period.

furyu. *fu* means "wind," and *ryu* means "to flow." A flowing through life which is not obvious.

haiku. a seventeen-syllable poetic form in the pattern 5, 7, 5.

hara. literally, "the belly"; the center point of one's body, found two to four inches below the navel. It is held to be the central reservoir of *ki* energy within a human being. The exact location is not on the surface of the skin, but is located two or three inches inside the lower abdomen.

harai. purity of body, mind, and heart.

ichigo-ichi-e. one time, one place: literally, "one encounter in one period." It means to take each encounter, each occasion, seriously, as if it were to happen only once in a lifetime.

iemoto. head person, ruler, leader, or the most accomplished.

inochi. the lifeforce, for example, of a flower.

ishitatesō. stone-laying monks.

jiriki. self-power: as in Zen Buddhist teaching, spiritual advancement is achieved by one's own efforts, one's own power.

kami. the Shintō term for the "divine." It is often translated as "god," but more accurately it refers to the mysterious, awesome, creative energy of the universe.

kannagara no michi. the flow of creative energy in the universe.

kansha. the spirit of thankfulness.

kare sansui. the dry-landscape garden.

keikō. training; a shorter-term, specifically focused form of development, rather than a lifelong practice (see *shugyō*) which aims at the self-cultivation of body, mind, and spirit.

kendō. the Way of the Sword; swordsmanship.

kenshin. a total offering of self.

kenshō. seeing's one's true nature; an initial enlightenment experience (see *satori*).

ki. "spirit," "life," "breath," universal (psychophysical) energy. Within a human being, *ki* energy follows the meridians as identified by acupuncture.

kiatsu. the healing application of *ki* energy in *aikidō.*

kisei. the tension among a garden's elements that creates energy.

kōban. the corner police box.

kodō. the Way of Incense.

kokoro. mind/heart; the showing of human-heartedness without an ulterior motive.

makoto. sincerity, integrity, truthfulness, honesty.

michi. the flow of creative energy of the cosmos; the sacred blood, energy, or spirit of the cosmos. *Michi* is the Way of the Universe, and one who has *michi* flows with the universe. It also means to have integrity, and indicates that one is linked with the "great All."

misogi. acts of purification; most often accomplished by means of cold water splashed on one's body, or by standing under an ice-cold waterfall.

mono no aware. Motoori Norinaga (1730–1801) used this term to refer to "the pathos of life" (literally, "the sorrow of things"). It is not a negative but a positive term reminding each of us that the transiency of all things should only make them more precious in our eyes. The term refers to aesthetic sensitivity as an awareness of the richness and diversity of life where beauty and sadness as the awareness of the fleeting quality of all things meet.

morotomo. to be together with; a relational indicator.

mu. nothingness, emptiness.

mushin. no-mind.

naginata. a lance, or a sword on a pole, usually used by women; it has a crescent shaped blade.

nembutsu. "calling the name" of Buddha; central feature of Pure Land Buddhism.

nirvāna. Sanskrit: blown out, or cooled; to blow off, as one would blow out the flame of a candle, i.e., to extinguish a tendency which recurs in the samsaric world. Becoming free of the three poisons; greed (mostly sexual impulse), hatred (anger), and delusion (foolishness). Ultimate reality. Realizing the unreality of self and world which we ordinarily take as reality.

o'hana-mi. the seasonal viewing of flowers.

Ōmoto-kyo. a religious (Shintō) sect with which Ueshiba-sensei was first associated. Deguchi Ōnisaburō was a key teacher of this sect.

onegai shimasu. please; please do me a favor; please teach me; please practice with me. It is an expression used when politely asking someone to do something.

raku. a rustic style of Japanese pottery developed at a Zen temple in Kyoto, when Sen no Rikyū asked a Korean potter to make pottery using the materials and techniques usually associated with the making of roof tiles.

renga. a form of Japanese poetry consisting of a string of verses in the sequence of 5, 7, 5, and 7, 7 syllables per line.

rikka. a style of flower arranging. Literally, "standing up plant cuttings," which implies a decidedly vertical emphasis.

Rinzai Zen Buddhism (see Zen Buddhism).

sabi. an aesthetic principle of never forcing, never straining, like an old man making the effort to stand while at death's door. An aesthetic term used to designate something that gives the impression of being rustic.

sadō. the Way of Tea (see also *chadō* and *chanoyu*).

Sakuteiki. Japan's first, and best known, manual of landscape gardening.

samādhi. a Buddhist term meaning concentration or absorption; in the state of *samādhi*, there is a loss of self. In meditation, it is the state of fixing attention on a single object.

samsāra. this ordinary world, as contrasted with *nirvāna*, or seeing the world through enlightened eyes. It designates a cycle of birth and death and, by implication, it also means the empirical, phenomenal world. In Zen Buddhism, one comes to see that *samsāra* is *nirvāna*, and *nirvāna* is *samsāra*; that the everyday world is a manifestation of true reality, and that true reality is only to be found in the everyday world when it is viewed from the point of view of emptiness.

satori. illumination, enlightenment (see also *kenshō*).

seika tanden. the *hara.* *Ki* energy is centered in the lower abdomen, two or three inches below the navel. This energy reservoir is *seika tanden* (see *hara*).

seiza. a sitting posture, feet positioned under one's buttocks.

sensei. honored teacher; literally, "one who has gone before."

seppuku. ritual suicide.

shibui. studied restraint; to be understated.

shimenawa. a straw rope separating or marking off a rock, or a tree, or a waterfall, etc., as sacred, awesome, *kami*-infused.

shinai. the split bamboo practice "sword."

Shintō. the Way of the Gods; the indigenous religion of Japan which is a major source of those cultural and ethical teachings inherent to Japanese culture.

shōgun. a warlord. When the power of the Emperor waned, beginning in 1156, powerful local rulers emerged, and a system of feudal rule was established in 1192.

shugyō. sustained, committed, lifelong practice. The goal of *shugyō* is the self-transformation of body, mind, and spirit. It is to be contrasted with *keikō*, which is specific training in sport, or the training of specific muscle sets, or which refers to "this training session," and which tends to focus on the body.

Sōtō Zen Buddhism (see Zen Buddhism).

sumi-e. brush and ink drawing. Brush painting is another *dō*, whose aim it is to capture the essence of what is being painted. A handful of artfully accomplished brush strokes on simple rice paper can convey a complex landscape.

tariki. other-power. Saving grace and mercy are freely offered to those who simply call upon the name of Amida Buddha. One is saved not by self-effort (see *jiriki*) or works, but by the saving grace of Buddha alone. Grace is something given, not something earned.

tokonoma. a recessed part of a Japanese-style room, with a raised dias for a floor, and a lowered ceiling: a kind of alcove. It serves as the place where a scroll, a vase, and a small flower arrangement are brought together to comprise a decorative theme for a tea ceremony, or simply as an expression of the Japanese aesthetic sense.

wabicha. the rustic, simple *wabi*-style of serving tea.

waka. an early form of Japanese poetry consisting of a fixed number of syllables (5 or 7) per line. The usual form was a poem of five lines, with syllable counts of 5, 7, 5, 7, and 7.

Wakei No Niwa. the Zen garden at the Museum of Civilization in Hull, Quebec, Canada (Ottawa), designed and installed by Masuno Shunmyo. The title means "to understand and respect all cultures."

yūgen. the incompleteness that triggers the emotions of melancholy and sadness; the profound suggestibility of things. Falling leaves herald the onset of a cold and lifeless winter: happiness is transient and will give way to something else. But *yūgen* also identifies a deep profundity by encouraging the mindful appreciation of the beauty, happiness, and good health that, for the moment, exists. All beauty of worth is fleeting, rendering it all the more precious.

zazen. Zen meditation while sitting in an appropriate posture. The aim of *zazen* is *satori*.

Zen Buddhism. the two major schools of Zen Buddhism are Rinzai and Sōtō. Rinzai Zen came to Japan in 1191 by the monk Eisai; Dōgen introduced Sōtō Zen to Japan in 1227.

Rinzai Zen's training focus is on *kōans*, teaching stories that appear to be insoluble puzzles. Through unrelenting concentration on such puzzles, it is hoped that the student will advance beyond conceptual thinking to an instant realization that is *satori*. D. T. Suzuki, who introduced Zen to the West, wrote almost exclusively of Rinzai Zen.

Sōtō Zen's training is largely *zazen* or seated meditation. Both schools employ *kōans* and *zazen*, but not only is the emphasis different, Sōtō Zen teaches that the purpose of meditation is not some distant *satori*, but rather that *satori* is the very act of meditating, as are all other acts which are undertaken mindfully as events along a path seriously followed. In this sense, the path to *satori* is gradual, rather than sudden, and already present all along the way. Enlightenment is not a single great event, but the sustained choice to follow the path of meditation and practice.

REFERENCES

Berthier, François. 2000. *Reading Zen in the Rocks: The Japanese Dry Landscape Garden*, trans. and with a philosophical essay by Graham Parkes. Chicago: University of Chicago Press.

Buber, Martin. 1958. *I and Thou*, trans. Ronald Gregor. New York: Scribner.

Carter, Robert E. 1992. *Becoming Bamboo: Western and Eastern Explorations of the Meaning of Life*. Montreal and Kingston: McGill-Queen's University Press.

————. 1997. *The Nothingness Beyond God: An Introduction to the Philosophy of Nishida Kitarō*, second edition. St. Paul, Minnesota: Paragon House.

————. 2001. *Encounter with Enlightenment: A Study of Japanese Ethics*. Albany: State University of New York Press.

Chuang Tzu [now Zhuangzi]. 1964. *Chuang Tzu: Basic Writings*, trans. Burton Watson. New York: Columbia University Press.

Coe, Stella. 1984. *Ikebana: A Practical Guide to Japanese Flower Arrangement*, ed. M. L. Stewart. New York: Gallery Books.

Dale, Peter N. 1991. *The Myth of Japanese Uniqueness*. New York: Palgrave Macmillan, Reprint Edition.

Davey, H. E. 1999. *Brush Meditation: A Japanese Way to Mind and Body Harmony*. Berkeley: Stone Bridge Press.

————, and Ann Kameoka. 2000. *The Japanese Way of the Flower: Ikebana as Moving Meditation*. Berkeley: Stone Bridge Press.

———. 2003. *Living the Japanese Arts and Ways: 45 Paths to Meditation and Beauty*. Berkeley: Stone Bridge Press.

Deshimaru, Taisen. 1991. *The Zen Way to the Martial Arts*, trans. Nancy Amphoux. New York: Arkana, Penguin Books.

Deutsch, Eliot. 1975. *Studies in Comparative Aesthetics*, Monographs of the Society for Asian and Comparative Philosophy, no. 2. Honolulu: University of Hawaii Press.

Dōgen. 1985. *Moon in a Dewdrop: Writings of Zen Master Dōgen*, ed. Kazuaki Tanahashi. San Francisco: North Point Press.

———. 1997. "Keiseisanshoku" (Sounds of the valley, color of the mountains) [also translated as "Valley Sounds, Mountain Sights"], in *Shōbōgenzō*, trans. K. Nishiyama and J. Stevens, 4 vols. Sendai: Daihokkaikaku, 1975–83. Quoted in Parkes 1997, p. 117.

Dumoulin, Heinrich. 1979. *Zen Enlightenment: Origins and Meaning*, trans. John C. Maraldo. New York: Weatherhill.

———. 1992. *Zen Buddhism in the Twentieth Century*, trans. J. S. O'Leary. New York: Weatherhill.

Faure, Bernard. 1993. *Chan Insights and Oversights: An Epistemological Critique of the Chan Tradition*. Princeton: Princeton University Press.

Forman, Robert K. C. 1999. *Mysticism, Mind, Consciousness*. Albany: State University of New York Press.

Freeman, Michael, and Michiko Rico Nosé. 2002. *The Modern Japanese Garden*. Boston: Tuttle Publishing.

Fujisawa, Chikao. *Some Parapsychological Aspects of Shintō* (mimeographed). Cited in Herbert 1967, p. 21.

Fung Yu-lan. 1953. *A History of Chinese Philosophy*, 2 vols. Princeton: Princeton University Press.

Gleason, William. 1995. *The Spiritual Foundations of Aikidō*. Rochester, Vermont: Destiny Books.

Hammitzsch, Horst. 1988. *Zen in the Art of the Tea Ceremony.* New York: E. P. Dutton.

Heisig, James W., and John C. Maraldo, eds. 1994. *Rude Awakenings: Zen, the Kyoto School, and the Question of Nationalism.* Honolulu: University of Hawaii Press.

Herbert, Jean. 1967. *Shintō: At the Fountain-Head of Japan.* London: George Allen and Unwin Ltd.

Herrigel, Eugen. 1971. *Zen in the Art of Archery.* New York: Vintage Books.

Herrigel, Gustie L. 1987. *Zen in the Art of Flower Arrangement,* trans. R. F. C. Hull. London: Arcana.

Hirota, Dennis, ed. 1995. *Wind in the Pines: Classic Writings of the Way of Tea as a Buddhist Path.* Fremont, California: Asian Humanities Press.

Hisamatsu, Shin'ichi. 1982. *Zen and the Fine Arts,* trans. G. Tokiwa. Tokyo: Kodansha International Ltd.

Hoover, Thomas. 1977. *Zen Culture.* New York: Vintage Books.

Hyams, Joe. 1982. *Zen in the Martial Arts.* Toronto: Bantam Books.

Ives, Christopher. 1992. *Zen Awakening and Society.* Honolulu: University of Hawaii Press.

Kadowaki, Kakichi, S. J. 1993. "Shintō and Christianity: Dialogue for the Twenty-First Century," *International Philosophical Quarterly* 33, no. 1 (March 1993), pp. 70–89.

Kamata, Shigeo, and Shimizu Kenji. 1992. *Zen and Aikidō.* Tokyo: Aiki News.

Kim, Hee-Jin, trans. 1985. *Flowers of Emptiness: Selections From Dōgen's Shōbōgenzō,* Studies in Asian Thought and Religion, Volume 2. Lewiston/Queenston: The Edwin Mellen Press.

Koren, Leonard. 1994. *Wabi-Sabi for Artists, Designers, Poets and Philosophers.* Berkeley: Stone Bridge Press.

Leach, Bernard. 1975. *Hamada: Potter.* Tokyo: Kodansha International Ltd.

Marra, Michael F., ed. 2002. *Japanese Hermeneutics: Current Debates on Aesthetics and Interpretation.* Honolulu: University of Hawaii Press.

Masuno, Shunmyo. 1995. "Landscapes in the Spirit of Zen: A Collection of the Work of Shunmyo Masuno. *Process Architecture*, Special Issue 7.

———. 1999. *Ten Landscapes*, ed. J. G. Trulove. Rockport, Massachusetts: Rockport.

Mayeroff, Milton. 1971. *On Caring.* New York: Perennial Library, Harper and Row.

Miyamoto, Musashi. 1974. *A Book of Five Rings (Go Rin no Sho)*, trans. Victor Harris. Woodstock, New York: The Overlook Press.

Morita, Kiyoko. 1999. *The Book of Incense: Enjoying the Traditional Art of Japanese Scents.* Tokyo: Kodansha International.

Nishida, Kitarō. 1976. *Intelligibility and the Philosophy of Nothingness: Three Philosophical Essays*, trans. Robert Schinzinger. Westport, Connecticut: Greenwood Press.

———. 1990. *An Inquiry into the Good*, trans. M. Abe and C. Ives. New Haven: Yale University Press.

Nishitani, Keiji. 1995. "The Japanese Art of Arranged Flowers," trans. Jeff Shore in Chapter 1, "Japanese Philosophy," by Graham Parkes, in Robert C. Solomon and Kathleen M. Higgins, eds., *World Philosophy: A Text with Readings.* New York: McGraw-Hill, pp. 23–27.

———. in preparation. *Contemporary Problems and Religion*, trans. S. Yamamoto and R. E. Carter.

Nitobe, Inazo. 1969. *Bushidō: The Soul of Japan.* Rutland, Vermont: Charles E. Tuttle.

Parkes, Graham. 1997. "Voices of Mountains, Trees, and Rivers: Kukai, Dōgen, and a Deeper Ecology," in M. E. Tucker and D. R. Williams, eds., *Buddhism and Ecology: The Interconnection of Dharma and Deeds.* Cambridge, Massachusetts: Distributed by the Harvard University Press for the Harvard University Center for the Study of World Religions.

———. 2002. "The Eloquent Stillness of Stone: Rock in the Dry Landscape Garden," in Michael F. Marra, ed., *Japanese Hermeneutics: Current Debates on Aesthetics and Interpretation.* Honolulu: University of Hawaii Press, pp. 44–59.

Picken, Stuart D. B. 1994. *Essentials of Shintō: An Analytical Guide to Principal Teachings.* Westport, Connecticut: Greenwood Press.

Plato. 1956. *Plato's Protagoras,* ed. Gregory Vlastos. Indianapolis: A Liberal Arts Press Book, The Bobbs-Merrill Co.

———. 1964. *The Collected Dialogues of Plato: Including the Letters,* Bollingen Series LXXI, ed. E. Hamilton and H. Cairns. New York: Pantheon Books.

Reed, William. 1992. *A Road That Anyone Can Walk: Ki.* Tokyo and New York: Japan Publications.

Reid, T. R. 1999. *Confucius Lives Next Door: What Living in the East Teaches Us About Living in the West.* New York: Random House.

Saotome, Mitsugi. 1993. *Aikidō and the Harmony of Nature.* Boston and London: Shambhala.

Sato, Hiroaki. 1986. *The Sword and the Mind.* Woodstock, New York: The Overlook Press.

Sen, Soshitsu [Genshitsu is his retirement name]. 1979a. *Chadō: The Japanese Way of Tea.* New York: Weatherhill/Tankosha.

———. 1979b. *Tea Life, Tea Mind.* New York: Weatherhill. Published for the Urasenke Foundation, Kyoto.

———. 1998. *The Japanese Way of Tea: From Its Origins in China to Sen Rikyū,* trans. V. D. Morris. Honolulu: University of Hawaii Press.

Shaner, David Edward. 1985. *The Bodymind Experience in Japanese Buddhism: A Phenomenological Study of Kūkai and Dōgen.* Albany: State University of New York Press.

Solomon, Robert C., and Kathleen M. Higgins, eds. 1995. *World Philosophy: A Text with Readings.* New York: McGraw Hill.

Stevens, John. 1987. *Abundant Peace: The Biography of Morihei Ueshiba, Founder of Aikidō.* Boston: Shambhala.

———. 1995. *The Secrets of Aikidō.* Boston: Shambhala.

———. 2001. *The Philosophy of Aikidō.* Tokyo: Kodansha International.

Stone, John, and Meyer, Ron, eds. 1995. *Aikidō in America.* Berkeley: Frog.

Suzuki, Daisetz T. 1959. *Zen and Japanese Culture*, Bollingen Series LXIV. Princeton: Princeton University Press.

———. 1963. *Outlines of Mahāyāna Buddhism.* New York: Shocken Books.

———. 1970. *Shin Buddhism: Japan's Major Religious Contribution to the West.* London: George Allen and Unwin.

Takei, J., and M. P. Keane, trans. 2001. *Sakuteiki: Visions of the Japanese Garden.* Boston: Tuttle.

Takuan, Sōhō. 1987. *The Unfettered Mind: Writings of the Zen Master to the Sword Master*, trans. W. S. Wilson. Tokyo: Kodansha International.

Teeuwen, Mark. 1996. "Western Understanding and Misunderstanding of Shintō: Progress of Studies on Shintō in the West and Some Remarks," in *International Symposium Commemorating the Founding of the International Shintō Foundation: Shintō—Its Universality.* Tokyo: International Shintō Foundation, pp. 76–82.

Tohei, Koichi. 1961. *Aikidō: The Coordination of Mind and Body for Self-Defence.* Tokyo: Rikugei Publishing House.

———. 1962. *What Is Aikidō?* Tokyo: Rikugei Publishing House.

———. 1966. *Aikidō in Daily Life.* Tokyo: Rikugei Publishing House.

———. 1996a. "Interview with Koichi Tohei (1)," by Stanley Pranin, *Aikidō Journal*, no. 107.

———. 1996b. "Interview with Koichi Tohei (2)," by Stanley Pranin, *Aikidō Journal*, no. 109 (Fall/Winter).

———. 1997. "Interview with Koichi Tohei (3)," by Stanley Pranin, *Aikidō Journal*, no. 111.

———. 2001a. *The Way to Union with Ki: Aikidō with Mind and Body Coordinated*, trans. William Reed. Utsonomiya, Tochigi: Ki no Kenkyukai Headquarters.

———. 2001b. *Ki in Daily Life*, Complete Revised Edition. Utsonomiya, Tochigi: Ki no Kenkyukai Headquarters.

Tsunoda, R., W. T. DeBary, and Donald Keene. 1964. *Sources of Japanese Tradition*. New York: Columbia University Press.

Ueshiba, Kisshomaru. 1987. *The Spirit of Aikidō*. Tokyo: Kodansha International.

Ueshiba, Morihei. 1991. *Budō: Teachings of the Founder of Aikidō*. Tokyo: Kodansha International.

———. 1992. *The Art of Peace*, trans. John Stevens. Boston: Shambhala.

———. 1993. *The Essence of Aikidō: Spiritual Teachings of Morihei Ueshiba*, ed. John Stevens. Tokyo: Kodansha International.

Victoria, Brian Daizen. 1997. *Zen at War*. New York: Weatherhill.

Warner, G., and D. F. Draeger. 1983. *Japanese Swordsmanship: Technique and Practice*. New York: Weatherhill.

Watsuji, Tetsurō. 1996. *Watsuji Tetsurō's Rinrigaku: Ethics in Japan*, trans. S. Yamamoto and R. E. Carter. Albany: State University of New York Press.

Yanagi, Sōetsu. 1972. *The Unknown Craftsman: A Japanese Insight into Beauty*. Tokyo: Kodansha International.

Yuasa, Yasuo. 1987. *The Body: Toward an Eastern Mind-Body Theory*, ed. T. P. Kasulis, trans. S. Nagatomo and T. P. Kasulis. Albany: State University of New York Press.

———. 1993. *The Body, Self-Cultivation, and Ki-Energy*, trans. S. Nagatomo and M. S. Hull. Albany: State University of New York Press.

INDEX

163